LINDA HANTRAIS

G000164754

WHAT BREXIT MEANS FOR EU AND UK SOCIAL POLICY

POLICY PRESS SHORTS POLICY & PRACTICE

First published in Great Britain in 2019 by

Policy Press
University of Bristol
1-9 Old Park Hill
Bristol
BS2 8BB
UK
t: +44 (0)117 954 5940
pp-info@bristol.ac.uk
www.policypress.co.uk

North America office:
Policy Press
c/o The University of Chicago Press
1427 East 60th Street
Chicago, IL 60637, USA
t: +1 773 702 7700
f: +1 773 702 9756
sales@press.uchicago.edu
www.press.uchicago.edu

© Policy Press 2019

British Library Cataloguing in Publication Data
A catalogue record for this book is available from the British Library.

Library of Congress Cataloging-in-Publication Data
A catalog record for this book has been requested.

ISBN 978-1-4473-3715-7   (paperback)
ISBN 978-1-4473-3717-1   (ePub)
ISBN 978-1-4473-3718-8   (Mobi)
ISBN 978-1-4473-3716-4   (ePDF)

Cover design by Policy Press
Printed and bound in Great Britain by CMP, Poole
Policy Press uses environmentally responsible print partners

Contents

Abbreviations

CEE	Central and Eastern Europe
CJEU	Court of Justice of the European Union
DG	Directorate-General
ECSC	European Coal and Steel Community
EESC	European Economic and Social Committee
EEA	European Economic Area
EC	European Communities
EEC	European Economic Community
EMPL	Directorate-General for Employment, Social Affairs and Inclusion
EMS	European Monetary System
EMU	Economic and Monetary Union
EPP	European People's Party
ERDF	European Regional Development Fund
ERM	Exchange Rate Mechanism
ESF	European Social Fund
EU	European Union
FP	Framework Programme for research
OMC	Open Method of Coordination
QMV	Qualified majority voting
RTD	Directorate-General for Research and Innovation
SEA	Single European Act
SIP	Social Investment Package
TFEU	Treaty on the Functioning of the European Union
TUC	Trades Union Congress
UKIP	UK Independence Party

Preface

In many respects *What Brexit means for EU and UK social policy* is a sequel to my three editions of *Social policy in the European Union*, the last of which was published in 2007 when the European Union was 50 years old. The focus in each of the editions was on the interactive multi-level relationship between EU institutions and national governments. The chapters spanned working and living conditions, education, family and gender issues, old age, social inclusion and migration. On the eve of the global financial crises, it could be demonstrated that few areas of social life remained untouched by European regulations, directives, decisions, recommendations, resolutions, communications or memoranda, social action programmes and white papers.

Although the UK was not the only member state concerned about the pervasiveness of the EU's powers, or to be affected by euroscepticism, the general tone of EU policy statements remained positive. Transforming the socio-economic and technological changes taking place in the early years of the 21st century from obstacles into opportunities was considered challenging but not impossible. Action plans were being prepared to deliver a concerted strategy to secure the future viability of social protection systems, based essentially on the creation of more and better jobs, and longer working lives of better quality.

The 10 years from 2007 to 2017 created new hurdles, as the global financial crisis was followed first by the eurozone crisis, and then by the refugee crisis. Although the UK was not in the eurozone or in Schengen, it could not avoid the destabilising effects of the crises on public finances and the ensuing years of austerity. The loss of trust in the ability of government at national and EU levels to deal with the aftermath of the crises was an important factor driving the decision in the 2016 referendum to withdraw from the EU.

This book argues that the seeds of euroscepticism and Brexit were sown long before the crises and that the UK was never fully committed or emotionally attached to the EEC founding members' vision of economic and political union. Rather, during its membership, the approach of UK governments was most often transactional as they opposed any formalisation of social union.

The justification for producing this account of Europe's social dimension in the context of Brexit is to consider in more detail the UK's perspective on EU social policy development and the role that it played in both promoting and hindering European social integration. The UK took 10 years to join the EEC, and it could be 10 years or more before a meaningful assessment can be made of the impact for EU and UK social policy of the UK's decision to leave the EU.

This book draws on a wider range of resources than in the three editions of *Social policy in the European Union*, including official documents, political biographies and speeches, critical political and social science literature, media reports and blogs. To assist readers in following the chronology of events and legislation, the book contains a social policy timeline in addition to the list of references cited in the text.

I am grateful to the many colleagues who reviewed drafts of the book for their insightful comments and advice. Any errors of interpretation remain my own.

Linda Hantrais

ONE

Introduction

Social policy has long been a contested area for European institutions, member states, their governments and their electorates. While the UK's withdrawal negotiations focussed primarily on trade, arguably social issues played a significant role in persuading a majority of electors in the UK to vote leave in the 2016 referendum on Europe, as well as being a determining factor in the decision of many of those who voted to remain.

What Brexit means for EU and UK social policy draws on a range of disciplinary, conceptual and theoretical approaches to analyse and understand the complex interconnections between social policy formation, implementation and governance at European and national levels. The book highlights the social issues, debates and policy challenges facing Europe at different stages in its development over the 60 years since the establishment of the European Economic Community (EEC) in 1957.

The European Union (EU), as it is known since the 1992 Maastricht Treaty, has had to accommodate an ever greater diversity of welfare arrangements. Member states have sought to deal collectively with the social implications of population ageing, technological change, global financial, eurozone and refugee crises, and the fallout from international conflicts. With Brexit, arguably, as one of the greatest challenges in the EU's history, this book seeks to understand what the results of the 2016 referendum might mean for EU and UK social policy, by exploring five key questions:

- what is meant by social policy and, more specifically, by European social policy;
- why the EEC had a social dimension and what its characteristics were;
- how the concept of European social policy evolved and changed during the 45 years of the UK's membership;
- how social policy became an issue in the 2016 referendum campaign and the withdrawal negotiations;
- what impact Brexit might have on the future development of social policies at EU and national levels.

The book adopts a thematic and chronological approach in undertaking a systematic review of the debates surrounding the social dimension and its place in the European project. It scrutinises evidence in support of claims that successive UK governments have both hindered and encouraged social policy development within the EU, acknowledging that the ambivalent role played by the UK makes it difficult to predict the medium and longer term effects of the Brexit vote for EU and UK social policy.

This introductory chapter opens discussion of the first of the five framing questions by examining the many meanings attributed to social policy and, more specifically, to European social policy. The chapter identifies and contextualises the multifarious disciplinary and national approaches to the analysis and development of social policy in Europe, before reviewing the themes that run throughout the book and summarising the chronological structure of the chapters as they explore the other four key questions.

Conceptualising social policy

The meanings attributed to social policy are many and varied. Social scientists at national and EU levels disagree about whether social policy is a discipline in its own right or a cross-cutting field of research attracting scientists from different disciplines, ranging across history, politics, economics, sociology and law (Hudson and Lowe, 2004: 253). These disciplinary approaches can be mutually challenging and potentially cross-fertilising, particularly when viewed from a comparative international perspective (Clasen, 2013: 72–3). Additionally, in the literature and in practice, social policy is rarely recognised as an autonomous field of advanced study outside the English-speaking world. More often it is considered as a subset of 'public policy', meaning any policy formulated by government, be it environment, energy or, especially, taxation policy. Social policy is often juxtaposed with taxation policy in political statements indicating their conceptual and practical interconnectedness (Heath, 1972; Wilson, 1974; Blair, 1997; May, 2018).

The concept of 'welfare' is used both interchangeably with social policy and as a subarea of social policy targeting low-income groups (Hills, 2016). From an early focus essentially on poverty and redistribution of income, today in most advanced societies, the welfare domains routinely covered by social policy analysts extend beyond income maintenance and social security to employment, health and social care, public health, education, lifelong learning and housing (Alcock et al, 2016).

Welfare is also construed to comprise a wider range of social mechanisms beyond government, involving family, market, religious, non-governmental and other private organisations (Pierson, 2006; Burchardt and Obolenskaya, 2016). These agents were the main providers of welfare before the advent of the 'welfare state' (Manning, 2016: 22), the term widely used to describe the functions of governments as suppliers of social services and benefits on the basis of need. 'State welfare' refers to delivery by the state as distinct from commercial, voluntary and informal provision (Bochel, 2016).

'Social protection' is the term most often found in continental and non-Anglo-Saxon international literature to describe social policy or welfare provisions. The International Labour Organisation (ILO, 2000: 113), due to its primary concern with the interests of workers, juxtaposes social policy and social protection, thereby implying that they are conceptually different. Social protection in this case means social provisioning systems targeting the weakest members in society, whereas social policy refers to the wider policymaking framework.

Whether they adopt a social policy, social welfare, social protection, or public policy perspective and related terminology, social scientists share an interest in the theory and practice of welfare governance and arrangements. They examine the social wellbeing of citizens, as provided for in different socio-economic and political contexts through a wide variety of benefits and services (Kleinman and Piachaud, 1993: 3; Alcock, 2016: 7–8).

Conceptualising social policy in the European Union

European documents tend not to refer to public policy or social welfare, but to social policy in the generic sense, or to social protection. The main concern of the lawyers who drew up the regulatory texts on European treaties was to establish the legal instruments needed to deliver provisions that would advance social progress within European member states (Moussis, 2016: 13.5.3). Interpreted in a narrow sense, social policy, as defined in the 1957 Treaty of Rome establishing the EEC (articles 48–51 and 117–22), meant: measures to improve the living and working conditions of labour (117), close collaboration in the social field (118), non-discrimination in access to employment-related social security benefits for migrant workers and their families (51, 121), equal remuneration between women and men (119), and the maintenance of existing paid holidays (120). Only in the case of free movement of workers was provision made for legal instruments, such as directives and regulations (49) to implement policy. For other categories of beneficiaries, national law continued to take precedence. Only in the case of the European Social Fund (ESF) (123–8) was a dedicated European-managed and partially European-funded scheme envisaged as a redistributive mechanism to support re-employment and geographical mobility.

A conceptual link was made in the EEC Treaty to education and training (118), and to public health (48), leaving the way open for European-level initiatives to spill over into other social domains. Progressively, social protection assumed a broader sense in European law. It came to mean not only social security for migrant workers but an array of social rights for all citizens residing in EU member states, as laid down in the Charter of Fundamental Rights of the European Union, proclaimed in 2000. The original narrow designation of EEC social policy essentially as employment-related social protection led to the coupling of social and employment policy in later references to European social policy, exemplified in reports written for UK policy audiences (HM Government, 2014b).

Recognition of the centrality of employment in the conceptualisation of European social policy is also reflected in the development of the European Commission's organisational structure. A directorate-general (originally designated DG V) was responsible for the area broadly described as 'social affairs'. Initially, DG V encompassed social policy, manpower, the social fund and occupational training, social security and social services. In 1967–70, the portfolio of the Commissioner for Social Affairs included 'personnel' and 'administration'. These two functions were replaced by 'transport' and 'budget' in 1970–73.

DG V underwent numerous changes to its title during the process of enlargement, and as the Commission extended its competences in the social area. When, in 1973, Denmark, Ireland and the UK joined what was by then the European Communities (EC), following the Merger Treaty, the social affairs brief was assigned to an Irish Commissioner, Patrick Hillery (1973–76). 'Employment' was moved from the Economic to the Social Affairs portfolio in 1977. When Ivor Richard, one of the UK's two Commissioners, was appointed for the period 1981–84, his portfolio was extended from 'employment and social affairs' to incorporate 'education and training'. Between 1985–99, 'competition', 'industrial relations', 'immigration and home affairs' were added and then removed from the social affairs portfolio. Two further Irish appointees filled that office in 1985–89 and 1993–99 during the Delors and Santer presidencies. 'Equal opportunities' was added in 2004 under Prodi, and then replaced by 'inclusion' under Barroso in 2010, reflecting changing social priorities, competences and the need to accommodate the EU's enlarging membership.

The DG's title in 2018 was Employment, Social Affairs and Inclusion (EMPL); employment had figured in its attributions almost throughout UK membership. By the 2010s, the EU's expanding social competence and priorities, and the arrival of new member states had justified the introduction of separate DGs to deal with other cross-cutting areas of policy relevant to this book: Education, Youth, Sport and Culture (EAC), Regional and Urban Policy (REGIO), Research and Innovation (RTD), Health and Food Safety (SANTE), and Migration and Home Affairs (HOME).

Analysing European social policy

This book adopts a range of disciplinary perspectives in analysing the many facets of social policy in the EU. Most definitions of social policy in the European context refer to an institutionalised form of international governance imposing regulatory standards on member states. However, social scientists have long disagreed about how to conceptualise and theorise European social policy. Historians, sociologists, political economists and lawyers have developed their own theories about the contribution of the social dimension to the construction of a European 'union'. Consensus across disciplines is more likely to be found in the recognition that the EU has not become an autonomous supranational welfare state modelled on national systems (Pollack, 1998).

During the UK's membership, EU competence in the social policy area encroached incrementally into all aspects of social life to the extent that, for lawyers, 'EU law is not only economic law, but also social law' (Lenaerts and Gutiérrez-Fons, 2017: 434). The pervasiveness of EU social law means that it has become almost impossible to talk about domestic law without reference to European legislation and the crucial role played by the Court of Justice of the European Union (CJEU) in scrutinising and interpreting social law.

If analysts are to appreciate the factors leading to European treaty change, in line with the arguments of the 'new' historical institutionalists in the 1990s, they need an in-depth understanding of how agency and structure shape social policy outcomes in member states and their interaction with EU institutions (Thelen and Steinmo, 1992). These arguments are also useful for an understanding of the pathways that led progressively to the UK's referendum on membership and interpretations of its results.

Unlike lawyers and historical institutionalists, sociologists have focussed their attention on critical theory in the context of social change in Europe, addressing issues such as social relations, European xenophobia, the democratic deficit and the future of Europe (Favell and Guiraudon, 2011; Outhwaite, 2012; Seidler, 2018). In the UK, Anthony Giddens (2006) was interested in identifying a body of social values as a distinguishing characteristic of a European social policy model that had been emerging since 1994. After the 2008 financial crisis, he argued that the European social model, if not dead, was in serious jeopardy (Giddens, 2014: 89).

The primary reason for initially including a social dimension in the EEC Treaty was to even out economic and social imbalances in member states. Political economists, political scientists, international relations and social policy analysts attribute the economic rationale for the inclusion of social provisions to their function in market making, correcting market failures or enhancing market efficiency (Streeck, 1995; Hoskyns, 1996; Bailey, 2017; Daly, 2017; De la Porte, 2017; Ferrera, 2017). They have therefore often concentrated on assessing the extent to which social policy contributes to European economic integration (Pierson and Leibfried, 1995b; Geyer, 2000; Hooghe and Marks, 2008; Schimmelfennig, Leuffen and Rittberger, 2015).

Policy analysts from whatever discipline have long recognised the complexity of the multi-tiered, multi-scalar interactive relationship between governments in member states and EU-level regulatory institutions, based on mainly shared or competing competences, requiring constant adaptation, consensus and compromise (Pierson and Leibfried, 1995a; Kazepov and Barberis, 2017; Kennett, 2017). This complexity explains why it is difficult to understand the social policymaking process, and to predict how the UK's decision to withdraw from the EU might affect future social policy development both at EU level and in member states.

Conceptualising social policy in EU member states

By the mid-1990s, the number of member states had increased to 15 as more Nordic and Southern countries joined the EU. Enlargement to Central and Eastern European (CEE) countries, and to Cyprus and Malta in the 2000s, brought 13 more countries. Each wave of enlargement extended the range of political and social systems, thereby complicating the process of coordinating social provisions across member states, as required in the EEC Treaty. While EU institutions sought to regulate standards and identify common targets, individual nation states strived to protect their power to determine whether, and if so how, they endorsed and implemented EU social legislation.

As social policy developed into an area of shared competence between EU institutions and member state governments, the supremacy of the CJEU over national jurisdictions increasingly came to be perceived as a major challenge to the sovereignty of national welfare states and their courts (Leibfried, 2015). The relentless centralisation of control was not, however, matched by the harmonisation of national welfare systems, as initially anticipated. European social policy cannot, therefore, be considered as an amalgam of national social protection systems forming a supranational welfare state or a social union. Member states have maintained the diversity of their systems regarding not only their financial resources but also 'their normative aspirations and institutional structures' (Scharpf, 2002: 666), justifying the continued distinction between 'European social policy' and 'social policy in the EU' (Hantrais, 2007).

This intra-European diversity is amply demonstrated in the data provided by the Mutual Information System on Social Protection (MISSOC). The European Social Protection Committee (an advisory body to the European Commission) established MISSOC as a central database for monitoring national systems in 1990. MISSOC collates regularly updated comparable information on social protection legislation, benefits and conditions in EU member states, the European Economic Area (EEA) – Iceland, Liechtenstein and Norway – and Switzerland. Its detailed descriptive information about social protection funding and provisions reveals the diversity and complexity of national systems, covering: healthcare, sickness, maternity/paternity, invalidity, old age, survivors, accidents at work, occupational diseases, family benefits and services, unemployment, guaranteed minimum resources and long-term care.

By 2003 before the CEE countries, Cyprus and Malta joined the EU, the printed version of the database for EU15 member states had already reached almost 700 A4 pages. With 28 member states, a searchable open access version of the database was made available online, allowing researchers, policymakers and practitioners to compare and contrast the intricacies of evolving national welfare provisions across an ever enlarging Union.

According to data from the common framework provided by the European System of Integrated Social Protection Statistics (ESSPROS) for 2016, across EU28, total expenditure on social protection from public and private sources represented the largest budget head with 28.2% of GDP. By far the most important area of social expenditure was old age, mainly comprising pensions, accounting for 40.1% of total expenditure on social protection benefits, followed by 29.5% on sickness/health care, 8.7% on family/children, and 4.7% on unemployment.

Using ESSPROS data for 2016, Figures 1 and 2 show how EU member states differ in the proportion of their GDP devoted to social protection expenditure and in the receipts from different sources. As illustrated in Figure 1, the ratio of social protection expenditure to GDP varied across EU member states from 34.3% in France to 14.6% in Romania. Twelve EU member states from the first four waves of membership devoted at least 25% of total GDP to social protection, while Ireland joined the lowest spenders in the countries in the fifth and sixth membership waves. In terms of spending per capita in purchasing power standards (PPS), Luxembourg displayed a particularly high rate, while the figures for the UK and Ireland, and the Southern and Eastern European countries were at the lower end of the range.

The structure of receipts by source used to finance social protection in relation to GDP also varied markedly within and between membership waves, as shown in Figure 2. Government contributions (mainly from taxation) constituted by far the largest component of receipts in 2016 in Denmark, and the smallest in Estonia. Employers made the largest contribution in France, and the smallest in Denmark. Protected persons contributed most in the Netherlands and least in Estonia. In relation to GDP, in 2016, total social protection receipts, including from other sources, were highest in Denmark (35.7%) and France (34.4%), and lowest in Ireland (16.4%), Latvia (15.4%) and Romania (15.1%). These findings demonstrate how much different member states are willing and able to devote to social protection.

Figure 1: Social protection expenditure in EU28 as a % of total GDP and per capita in PPS, 2016

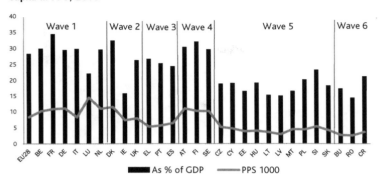

Source: European statistics explained: Social protection statistics, 2018

Figure 2: Social protection receipts in EU28 as a % of GDP, 2016

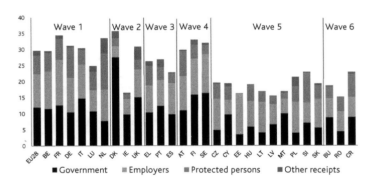

Source: European statistics explained: Social protection statistics, 2018

The analysis in the last two sections illustrates both the difficulties in delineating European social policy and the great diversity in the conceptualisation, organisation and delivery of national social protection systems, captured in the 1990s in a description of the relationship between national and supranational levels as 'complex, messy, and not well understood' (Streeck, 1995: 415).

Overview of themes

In considering the many configurations of social policy at EU and national levels, a number of recurring and interlocking themes can be identified. The following are most relevant to an understanding of why the UK public voted to leave the EU and the possible implications of that decision for the future development of social policy:

- the evolving relationship between the economic and social dimensions in EU policy development;
- the importance of protecting national interests and observing the principle of subsidiarity in the social domain;
- the changing distribution of social policy competences between EU institutions and member states;
- the shift from harmonisation of national systems to cooperation in recognition of national differences;
- the contribution of social policy to European integration.

From the outset, the social dimension was subordinated to the economic objectives of the EEC Treaty. Social policy was one of the EU's horizontal policies – with regional, taxation, competition and environment policy – supporting the goals set for economic and monetary union and political integration (Moussis, 2016: part IV). Harmonisation of social provisions was considered necessary to facilitate the free movement of workers between member states. From being a by-product of economic development, progressively social policy came to be portrayed as a productive

Policy chapter, just six articles were devoted to 'social provisions'. Social policy was assigned a limited, albeit specific, remit focussing on employment, and emphasising access to jobs for intra-European migrant workers, their working conditions and employment-related benefits. The European Commission's role was to monitor and report on the progress made in these areas, to initiate action programmes and bring forward policy proposals. Intra-European migration, access of migrants to national welfare benefits and the challenge to national sovereignty from allegedly overly powerful EU institutions were to become dominant issues in the UK referendum campaign.

Chapter 3 examines how the concept of European social policy evolved and changed during the 45 years of the UK's EC/EU membership. Initially, the UK had been reluctant to join the EEC. It was then thwarted in its attempts to become a member by French vetoes. As a condition of membership, with Denmark and Ireland, the UK parliament was obliged to give EC law supremacy over national law, by implementing all the primary and secondary social legislation that had previously been enacted. By the same token, EC membership in 1973 enabled the UK to participate actively in the decision-making process as the social dimension became a more important component of European integration. The UK was in a position both to encourage and hinder social progress. Despite the UK government's reputation as an 'awkward partner' (George, 1998), UK officials were recognised for their detailed scrutiny of European social legislation and their effective negotiating skills; and the UK was known to comply with EU laws once adopted (HM Government, 2014b: 56). UK appointees to the Commission and its committees, as well as policy advisers from the UK, made significant contributions to social policy development. The UK often uploaded national policies and provided examples of good policy practice (Hopkin and Van Wijnbergen, 2011). Based on such evidence, the UK's withdrawal might be expected to result in a loss for other member states. However, when the UK opted out of the Social Chapter in the 1992

Maastricht Treaty, the Commission exploited the opportunity to advance legislation that the UK government had previously blocked or delayed. With the UK permanently outside the EU, the Commission would be in a position to adopt similar tactics by bringing forward legislation that the UK could no longer contest.

Chapter 4 draws together the arguments explaining how social policy became an issue in the referendum campaign and the withdrawal negotiations. The UK's membership of the EC/EU coincided with a period during which the notion of social union, or social Europe, progressively moved on to the agenda, defined broadly as 'a union of national welfare states, with different historical legacies and institutions' (Vandenbroucke, 2017: 4). By the early 2000s, social policy spanned a wide range of benefits and services. The hostility of UK governments to EU intervention in national social affairs was fanned by the press and was reflected in public opinion. The level of contestation of European authority among political parties and electorates across the EU became more acute in the wake of the financial crisis, as did open expressions of euroscepticism and disaffection with the European project. The chapter shows how latent social issues came to the fore in determining voting patterns in the referendum and were salient in the withdrawal negotiations. In political speeches and white papers, Prime Minister Theresa May asserted that the UK would retain and enhance existing regulatory standards in the social domain. Whatever the nature of the future trading relationship and organisational links between the UK and its EU neighbours, in responding to public concerns, she remained adamant that the management of immigration and the social security rights of future EU migrants would no longer be under the control of the European courts.

Chapter 5 considers the stance adopted on social policy issues by EU institutions and member states in the withdrawal negotiations, and the possible implications of Brexit for the future development of EU-level social policy. The global financial and eurozone crises resulted in widespread welfare retrenchment, justifying enhanced EU-level coordination and solidarity as EU institutions sought to reassert their authority. The UK's decision to withdraw from the EU coincided with the rise to power of populist governments and the refugee crisis, which undermined the very premises on which the European social model had been constructed, arguably presenting a greater threat to EU social solidarity than Brexit. Even before the UK triggered article 50, the European Commission was advocating a more pro-active approach to future EU social policy to demonstrate to increasingly eurosceptic EU citizens that the Commission had not lost sight of their interests (Cooper, 2017). At the same time, EU27 negotiators were determined to ensure that the UK should not be seen to benefit from leaving the EU.

Chapters 2 to 5 tracked the chronological development of the EU's social dimension and the UK's contribution to European social integration during EC/EU membership, the referendum campaign and withdrawal negotiations. The concluding chapter returns to the themes recurring throughout the book and to the theoretical frameworks used to analyse and explain them. At critical stages in the EU's history, analysts have sought to predict how European social policy, or social policy in the EU, might develop in the future. In taking stock of past developments and future challenges, the chapter considers whether the official termination of the often troubled relationship between the UK and the EU would be likely to result in closer European social union or in social policy fragmentation and disintegration in the short and medium term. An open question for analysts is to what extent, in the longer term, UK governments might seek to disentangle and disconnect the UK from EU social legislation, and whether they will be in a position to use regained control over national social policy to focus attention on delivering the social progress demanded by a domestic audience.

TWO

Social policy in the EEC Treaty

The UK was not the only country to have doubts about surrendering control over national policymaking. In the early years of the European Economic Community (EEC), the French, under the presidency of Charles de Gaulle, were opposed to general economic integration. They wanted to protect national sovereignty, including in the social domain. They therefore rejected any major transfer of competence to a supranational institution. Since the UK government had been reluctant to enter into any commitment without knowing what the terms on offer meant or whether their national interests would be best served, Belgium, France, Germany, Italy, Luxembourg and the Netherlands had moved forward without the UK in launching a common market. At the outset, the UK thus forfeited the ability to influence the shape of European social policy during the EEC's formative years, foreshadowing its difficult relationship with European institutions and other member state governments in the decades to come.

Even before the EEC Treaty was agreed, the aspirant member states concluded that an interventionist social policy would be needed to avoid 'social dumping', if disparities in social protection provisions between member states were not to create an obstacle to mobility of labour and capital (Gold, 1993: 14). However, consensus was not easily achieved between the six founding member states on how such a social dimension should be framed and delivered. This chapter explains:

- why the EEC had a social dimension;
- what its characteristics were;
- why social policy was, from the outset, a contentious area;
- what the EEC/EU's social policy treaty commitments meant for the UK referendum and withdrawal negotiations.

These questions are examined with reference to the themes recurring throughout the book, namely: the relationship between the economic and social dimensions in European policy development; the efforts made by member states to safeguard national sovereignty over their social protection systems; the distribution of competences in the social domain between EU institutions and members states and the potential for their development; the associated shift from harmonisation of national systems to their coordination in recognition of national differences; and the contribution of UK social policy to European integration.

Justifying a social dimension in a common market

The Treaty of Rome was, by definition, primarily market driven. Social development was perceived as a cost factor or by-product of the economic dimension or, at most, a complement to it. A social dimension was accepted as a necessary but contentious area for inclusion in the EEC Treaty. The six founding member states were interested in the social dimension insofar as they considered it necessary to support economic growth and, especially, the free movement of workers, which was one of the Treaty's founding principles. This section explains why the original member states incorporated social provisions in the design of a common market, and why they are relevant to an understanding of Brexit.

Accommodating divergent approaches to social policymaking

Unlike federal states such as the US or Germany, the EU's constituent units in policymaking are national rather than subnational, and Europe's nation states have very different traditions for regulating welfare systems (Pierson and Leibfried, 1995a: 19). The EU lacks the financial resources of federal states, which helps to explain why it has relied heavily on regulatory policymaking requiring relatively little expenditure. The six EEC founding member states shared a common approach to industrial relations, with labour market legislation governing areas such as working time and employee representation. This commonality did not mean that they would find it easy to agree the size, shape and purpose of the rules governing social policy as an EEC Treaty commitment. It did mean that accommodating countries with different welfare traditions would be problematic.

The primary objective of the EEC founding member states was to facilitate postwar reconstruction and promote economic growth. The French argued that the high social charges the state imposed on employers and employees in the best interests of the workforce, combined with the principle of equal pay for men and women, which was written into the French constitution, would put France at a competitive disadvantage in relation to the other founding member states in achieving these objectives (Collins, 1975: 3–12). The French negotiators therefore advocated a 'level playing field' of competition, implying that everybody should be playing by the same rules with equal chances of success in the market place to avoid discrepancies in labour costs from distorting competition. They maintained that a higher level of social spending should be sought across member states to prevent those national governments wanting to introduce more generous provisions from being at a competitive disadvantage, exemplified by their measures for equalising pay between men and women (Hoskyns, 1996: 54–5). The French returned persistently to this theme during the Treaty negotiations arguing that they should not be penalised because of their higher social costs. They maintained that the other member states should align the costs of implementing equal pay, overtime and paid holidays with the levels applied for French workers.

The Germans countered the French case by contending that social charges were a result of the operation of market forces and should not be subject to regulation under EEC law. From the economic perspective, the Germans preferred a more liberal market system, and did not want to be forced to adopt French social charges. The Italians favoured a free labour market, harmonisation of social security contributions and a European fund to support the retraining and resettlement of workers (Collins, 1975: 6).

The search for compromise

In 1955, the six putative member states assigned Paul-Henri Spaak, the Belgian Foreign Minister and, subsequently, the Belgian signatory to the EEC Treaty, the task of forming an intergovernmental committee to draw up a report on the future EEC, including discussion of social issues. The report signalled the agreement among the six governments that the fusion of their markets 'would serve to eliminate wastage of resources and excessively high production costs' (Spaak, 1956: 2, 5). These benefits would, they believed, 'not be attainable unless transitional periods were granted, unfair competitive practices were stopped and governments cooperated in the quest for monetary stability, economic expansion and social progress'. To this end, the report also provided for an adaptation fund 'for the conversion of industrial plant and the retraining of workers' who were expected to be made redundant as a result of industrial restructuring.

In laying down the general principles underlying the EEC Treaty (Part One – Principles, article 2), its founders made a commitment to raise standards of living while also promoting 'closer relations' between member states. In seeking to achieve these objectives, they agreed, among others, to abolish obstacles to the free movement of persons, services and capital (article 3 §c), and to create a European Social Fund (ESF) to support unemployed workers through grants for vocational training and resettlement (article 3 §i). A compromise solution was reached whereby the EEC Treaty included a section on Social Policy (Part Three, Title III) without stipulating how most of the provisions should be implemented. Just six of the 248 articles in the Treaty were devoted to social provisions (articles 117–22). The remainder of the social policy articles (123–8) concerned the ESF.

The chapter on social provisions needs to be read in conjunction with other articles in the Treaty, particularly the 11 articles on freedom of movement for workers (Part Two, Title III, chapter 1, articles 48–51), cross-referenced in article 121 in the social policy section. Article 48 laid down the conditions for workers seeking employment in another member state. Measures to facilitate such free movement, which had been actively sought by the Italians, explicitly excluded employment in public administration in another member states, signalling their limited scope (article 48 §4). Article 51 provided for measures to be adopted in the field of social security for workers and their dependants resident in another member state to enable them to acquire and retain the right to payment of benefits.

Reconciling the social and economic dimensions

Together, these two sets of articles show how social policy was assigned a limited, albeit specific, remit: the focus was employment, emphasising access to jobs for intra-European migrant workers, their working conditions and employment-related benefits. Both the priorities of the founding member states and their existing regulatory systems were reflected in the employment-related provisions, summarised in article 118 as comprising: labour legislation and working conditions; occupational and continuation training; social security; protection against occupational accidents and diseases; industrial hygiene; the law as to trade unions, and collective bargaining between employers and workers.

The six articles (123–8) in the social provisions chapter setting out the arrangements for the ESF were designed to support geographical and occupational mobility of workers, and to relieve regional disparities. Article 125 specified, in more detail than for social provisions, the rules for granting assistance to enable the re-employment of workers.

Despite its limited legal instruments, the EEC Treaty provided the rationale for the Commission to play an active role in achieving social policy objectives. Accordingly, in its first annual report, the European Commission (1958: §§102, 103) placed these objectives 'on the same footing as those of economic character'. The Commission was aware that a large part of public opinion would judge the Community on the basis of its success in the social field.

Interest in the social dimension was boosted in 1965 when the EEC was merged with the European Coal and Steel Community (ESCS) and the European Atomic Energy Community (EAEC) to form the European Communities (EC). The ECSC had been established in 1951 to mitigate the impacts of industrial restructuring on displaced labour. It was, therefore, more purposefully concerned with social policy than the EEC Treaty. The ECSC was endowed with funds to cover the resettlement of displaced miners and steel workers and to promote improvements in their living and working conditions. Basic standards were laid down for the health and protection of workers and the general public, as well as procedures for monitoring and checking their implementation. The merger of the two treaties confirmed the economic justification for maintaining and strengthening the EEC Treaty's social dimension but did not give rise to any changes in the administrative procedures for implementing its principles. As in the ECSC, EEC Treaty provisions for social policy specifically targeted workers in the productive sector, while arrangements for redistributive benefits and public sector workers remained a matter for national welfare states.

Protecting national sovereignty over social systems

A shared belief among the EEC founding member states was that a step should be taken towards 'arrangements which would contain greater supra-national powers than those of the traditional international organization based on state co-operation' (Collins, 1975: 3). This section explores how they sought to balance control by national governments over their social policies with the centralising tendencies of EU institutions (Gold, 1993: 16–18).

Supranationalism vs national sovereignty

The founding member states differed in their approach to managing labour costs, and they disagreed about what was meant by supranationalism and how it should be achieved (Collins, 1975: 4–6). Due to opposition on the part of the French, any references to supranationalism in discussion documents needed to be accompanied by proposals for measures that would protect the French economy from competition. The Germans thought it unrealistic to hand over national responsibilities to a supranational institution, on grounds that the functions involved could not be split between different competences. The main objective for the Italians was political unity in Europe, with closer economic cooperation providing a stimulus for their economy, and migration easing unemployment. The Benelux countries supported 'linking further supra-nationalism with general economic integration in the form of a common market'; more specifically for the Dutch, 'the time was ripe for comprehensive economic integration amongst those countries willing to accept supra-national organization and provided measures were included to protect members against unfavourable economic and social repercussions'.

Spaak's main concern was not to create a supranational institution. He wanted to establish a common market as a first stage in a more fully integrated economy, where social protection was a factor in costs affecting competition, therefore requiring cooperation to achieve social progress. He foresaw the need to make provision for means of legal redress and parliamentary scrutiny. Based on the ECSC but less supranational in tone, the EEC Treaty (Part Five – Institutions of the Community, Sections 1–4) provided for an Assembly (later the European Parliament), Council (of Ministers), Commission and Court of Justice, each with its own attributions and competences. Their dependence on increasingly complex interactions between national and supranational actors with organised interests, subject to 'the dilemmas associated with institutions for shared policymaking', meant that European social policy merged with national social policy 'in an intricate process of competition, adjustment, and accommodation' (Pierson and Leibfried, 1995b: 433).

The limits of unanimous voting

Decisions in several areas in the social domain were dependent on unanimous voting, meaning that they would, in principle, remain under the control of national governments. The Spaak report (1956: 3) formulated 'a diffident invitation to establish supranational institutions', conceding with prescience that 'the rule requiring unanimity among the member governments might occasionally be waived'. Article 51, under the chapter on free movement of workers, defined as 'migrant workers and their beneficiaries', specified that: 'The Council, acting by means of a unanimous vote on a proposal of the Commission, shall, in the field of social security, adopt the measures necessary to effect the free movement of workers', enabling them to qualify for benefits according to 'the respective municipal law of the countries concerned' (51 §a). Article 121 in the chapter on social policy also stipulated that the Council, 'acting by means of a unanimous vote after consulting the Economic and Social Committee, may assign to the Commission functions relating to the implementation of common measures, particularly in regard to the social security of the migrant workers …'. Article 126 §b required a unanimous vote before any new tasks could be entrusted to the ESF within the framework of its mandate. The EEC Treaty thus incorporated what proved to be a fundamental but controversial principle – unanimity voting – in an area where it would be operationally difficult subsequently to apply European law without encroaching on national interests and sovereignty.

Closer reading of the social provisions for mobile workers demonstrates that the EEC Treaty already offered scope for overriding national sovereignty by presenting access as of right to social security not only for mobile workers but also for their beneficiaries resident in another member state (article 51). In setting a target date for the entry into force of freedom of movement of workers, article 48 §3c stipulated that arrangements should conform 'with the legislative and administrative provisions governing the employment of the workers of that State'. However, article 49 §§b, c went so far as to require progressive abolition of any locally applied administrative procedures and practices that might present obstacles to 'the freeing of movement of workers' or give rise to discrimination in access to employment.

By clearly setting out the implementation procedures for the social security of mobile workers and the standardisation of their working arrangements, article 49 thus provided the necessary means for overcoming the constraints of the unanimous voting rule, as implied by Spaak. In later years, the provisions in the EEC Treaty would pose an existential threat to national sovereignty in this area of social policy. They also added weight to the claims of Brexiteers seeking to 'regain control' over immigration.

increasingly into conflict with national policymakers, as the EC was enlarged, and the Commission's remit expanded.

Harmonising social policy

Although the Spaak report (1956: 5) referred only in general terms to the harmonisation of national legislation as a policy objective, the founding member states had announced in the Messina Declaration of June 1955 (predating the Spaak report), that they had agreed 'to take a new step on the road of European construction', starting with the economic sphere, and involving 'the gradual harmonisation of their social policies'. The Benelux countries had argued that social provisions for working hours, overtime and holiday pay should be harmonised. The French were advocating EEC-level legislation on equal pay, holiday pay and overtime, which they considered as areas of particular concern in protecting their labour force. The recommendation in the Messina Declaration (1955: 1, 2) was less ambitious, requiring 'study' rather than action, the aim being 'to improve steadily the living standard of the population'. This section examines why the objective of harmonising aspects of national social systems needed to be modified as new member states with different welfare arrangements joined the EEC.

Controversy over harmonisation

The EEC's dominant political philosophy was market driven. The founding member states held that, if enterprises could compete on equal terms, the distribution of resources would be optimised, enabling untrammelled economic growth, which would automatically result in social development, without the need for enforced harmonisation of national systems. With a view to ensuring that the assistance required would be available to help overcome its particular economic problems, Italy had argued for the harmonisation of taxes and social security, while also ensuring that the mechanics of free movement policy were properly worked out (Collins, 1975: 6). Social provisions as defined in the EEC Treaty were designed explicitly to underpin the principle stated in article 2 of raising living standards and promoting closer relations between its member states. Article 117 in the social provisions chapter set out, in somewhat obscure terms, the reasons for pursuing these objectives, as advocated by the French and the Germans:

Member States hereby agree upon the necessity to promote improvement of the living and working conditions of labour so as to permit the equalisation of such conditions in an upward direction.

They consider that such a development will result not only from the functioning of the Common Market which will favour the harmonisation of social systems, but also from the procedures provided for under this Treaty and from the approximation of legislative and administrative provisions. (EEC Treaty, article 117)

Harmonisation meant that national governments should accept certain common principles or adopt common standards in their social security systems. Elsewhere in the EEC Treaty (articles 100–2), provision was made to enable approximation of legislation when the Commission found that 'a disparity existing between the legislative or administrative provisions of the Member States distorts the conditions of competition'. Difficulties in reaching a consensus meant that other forms of cooperation progressively became necessary to prevent blockages.

Through collaboration and standardisation to coordination

Article 101 authorised the Council to issue directives, initially by unanimous voting, to eliminate disparities in provisions, whereas article 118 required only 'close collaboration between Member States in the social field'. No reference was made in the EEC Treaty to taxation and social contributions as a potential source of funding for social policy. The principle of equal pay without discrimination by sex was to be founded on work of 'equal value' (article 119), without specifying how these aims were to be achieved. Member states were to maintain 'existing equivalence of paid holiday schemes' (article 120). No mention was made of overtime and working hours, although the topic did return periodically to the social agenda. The EEC social provisions chapter thus left member states largely to decide which, if any, matters should be taken forward collectively (Collins, 1975: 23).

Implementation of the arrangements for mobile workers was more specific. Articles 56 §2 and 57 §1 enabled the Council to issue coordinating legislation for social provisions and for the mutual recognition of qualifications with the aim of facilitating the mobility of workers. Coordination, rather than harmonisation, of social security systems to protect migrant workers avoided the need to interfere with the autonomy of national governments over their social security systems.

In its first annual report on the activities of the Community, the European Commission (1958: §110) outlined its plans to harmonise professional classifications and employment services, in addition to setting up coordinating machinery for connecting offers of employment (§114). The Commission lost no time in addressing issues concerning industrial hygiene, medicine and safety (§121), including the standardisation of statistics on occupational accidents and diseases in collaboration with international and European specialist agencies. Social services, extending to living and housing conditions, were to be merely the subject of comparative 'studies' (§122).

In the decade following the establishment of the EEC, in areas where the Treaty made explicit provision for EEC institutions to intervene, the Commission brought forward legislation. Although the Treaty endowed the Commission with the powers needed to initiate the harmonisation of social protection systems, it could and did propose binding legislation, as noted above, for the coordination of social security systems for intra-European mobile workers. It also began to establish the administrative procedures required to operate the ESF, as permitted by the EEC Treaty in cooperation with the member states.

The EEC Treaty in practice

In a context of postwar reconstruction, the EEC Treaty established a customs union as the first stage in developing a common market preparing the way for a more fully integrated economy. Other longer term aims were to promote economic growth and achieve social progress. The first of the principles enshrined in the EEC Treaty was to work towards political unity by laying the foundations for 'an ever closer union among the European peoples'. The institutions created by the Treaty were designed to reach a balance between national and Community decision-making. From the outset, member states disagreed about not only the areas of social policy to be included but also the need for supranational institutions, the distribution of competences between such institutions and national governments, and the administrative procedures for achieving the objectives set. The compromise solution adopted by the signatories to the EEC Treaty was to incorporate a section on social policy but without stipulating how most of the provisions should be implemented.

The Commission's role was not to elaborate a European social policy, but to facilitate collaboration and mobility between member states. In the absence of unified taxation arrangements, the Community lacked the means to promote a fully funded redistributive EEC-level social policy. The key social policy article (117) in the EEC Treaty has been criticised for its looseness, obscurity and lack of regulatory precision and implementing procedures (Collins, 1975: 22). This 'cautious' approach to social affairs left national governments with the main responsibility for deciding where and how to act.

When the chapter on social provisions is read in conjunction with the articles on free movement of workers, a different picture emerges. The Treaty is much more specific about the measures needed to remove barriers to internal migration, since this was an area where national interests were more closely aligned. Nonetheless, the French initially expressed their concern about 'an excessive influx of Italians and of German refugees' (Collins, 1975: 13). By 1956, they had accepted the need for a policy on free movement of labour. The emphasis given in the Treaty to freedom of movement satisfied the Italians; they stood to benefit from the opportunities provided for accessing labour markets in other member states. The Germans realised that, as their economy revived, they would be suffering from labour shortages, and the Belgians were already aware of impending scarcities.

The most immediate beneficiaries from the EEC Treaty were the mobile workers who were able to seek and accept offers of employment anywhere in the Community. Under the terms of the Treaty (article 7), they could reside and work in another member state on the same conditions as the host population, without discrimination on grounds of nationality. The Commission started by developing close collaboration between employment services. These provisions were progressively extended to the self-employed during the 1960s and early 1970s. Attention was also paid to facilitating the exchange of young workers (article 50), and the Commission began work on a social action programme in consultation with the EESC.

International events and domestic upheavals meant that other areas of social policy were relatively neglected during the first decade of the EEC's existence, while the process was gradually phased in. However, social policy was destined to remain an area of conflict and divisiveness within and between EU member states, most notably regarding the integration of intra-European migrants, their access to national welfare benefits and the threat to national sovereignty from increasingly powerful European institutions. These issues were already a source of contention for the UK when it joined the EC. They were to become central concerns in the UK's referendum campaign four decades later.

THREE

UK influence on European social policy

In the aftermath of the Second World War, when plans were being discussed in 1947 for Europe's economic recovery, the UK declined an offer from the French to be involved in a project to form a European customs union. UK officials nonetheless took part in discussions in the 1950s with the six founding member states – Belgium, France, Germany, Italy, Luxembourg and the Netherlands – about proposals for economic integration. Due largely to its grave doubts about becoming a member of a supranational body, the UK's Conservative government left the talks that eventually led to the founding of a common market in 1957, thereby instigating what would subsequently be identified as 'the parting of the ways' (Young, 1989).

Even before the creation of the European Economic Community (EEC) and the failed attempts of the UK to join in the 1960s, evidence can be found of the conflictual relations existing among the potential member states over the social dimension. Efforts to reach consensus through trade-offs and compromise were further complicated by international and domestic events, and by clashes of personality and changing coalitions. Since the UK did not join the EEC during its formative years, not only did it forego an opportunity to influence the social dimension, but it was also unable to benefit from the favourable economic conditions enjoyed by the founding member states during the 1960s. By the time the UK joined what was by then the European Communities (EC) in 1973, it was engulfed in a global economic recession; and the UK's changing place in the world order was calling into question the role it might play in a European common market.

In seeking to gain a better understanding of the UK's influence on the development of EU social policy during its membership, this chapter addresses the following issues:

- how the accession of the UK affected the balance between the economic and social dimensions of the EC;
- how UK membership influenced the relationship and the distribution of competences between EU institutions and national governments in the social domain;
- how the UK assisted the European Commission in building its social policy capacity and the evidence base;
- how UK governments, officials and advisers encouraged and hampered the development of European social integration.

During its membership of the EC/EU, the same themes recurred as in the period before the UK joined. They serve here to frame the discussion: fluctuations in the priority given to social policy in relation to economic and political union, peaking during the disputes over the UK's budgetary rebate in the Thatcher years, the attempts to secure monetary union in the 1990s, and the aftermath of the 2008 financial crisis; the conflict between supranationalism and national sovereignty in the social domain as the social provisions of the EEC Treaty were progressively supplemented and implemented; associated issues over the sharing of competences between European institutions and member states; and continuing debates about the feasibility and desirability of harmonising social standards and coordinating social security systems.

Economic and social dimensions of UK membership

Before it became a member of the EC, the UK was already perceived as an 'awkward partner' and a 'stranger' in Europe (George, 1998; Wall, 2008). This section examines how the UK's membership of the EC/EU affected the evolving relationship between the social and economic dimensions of the EEC Treaty and, in particular, how UK politicians and officials promoted or hindered the development of social policy as a legitimate concern for member states.

Social policy on the European agenda

The welfare systems in the EEC founding member states have been described as 'traditionally passive, employment-based, status-preserving, social insurance and male-breadwinner orientated' (Hemerijck, 2017: 169). If Denmark, Ireland and the UK, with their different philosophies, traditions and legal practices, had become EC members in 1957, tensions would undoubtedly have been greater, and the debate about the regulatory framework would arguably have been even more controversial (Gold, 1993: 16–18).

In the early stages of the EEC's gestation, the UK was not in a position to block the social dimension, and, indeed, it pursued a policy of 'benevolence' towards the European project (Young, 1989: 198–9). The government was, however, fully aware of the issues being debated and the conflicting national interests that would need to be resolved. By distancing itself from the six founding member states, and by being distanced by them, the UK missed the opportunity to participate in the discussions that were shaping the Community and were destined to lead social policy in directions that successive UK governments would seek to moderate through a combination of formal negotiations, blocking tactics, opt-outs and trade-offs, often in cooperation with like-minded partners.

The accession of three new member states after nearly two decades of operation provided the Commission with an incentive to pool resources in seeking solutions to common social problems. The founding member states soon realised that economic expansion might not automatically result in an improved quality of life, contrary to the expectations underlying the EEC Treaty. While the UK was negotiating EC membership in 1972, in its role as a policy initiator the Commission was preparing a more broadly couched social action programme designed to recalibrate and rebalance the relationship between the economic and social dimensions. At the Paris summit of heads of state or government in 1972, the UK put down a marker by disagreeing with a proposal from Germany for a common social policy based on strengthening and centralising labour law. By contrast, the UK and Ireland joined Italy in supporting the creation of a European Regional Development Fund (ERDF) as a redistributive policy mechanism, in addition to the European Social Fund (ESF) which was written into the EEC Treaty (articles 123–8) (George, 1998: 58–60).

UK participation in EU social policymaking

As a full member of the EC in 1973, the UK had an opportunity to participate in the decision-making process at a time when the social dimension was becoming recognised as a more significant component of European integration. The ERDF had been scheduled to be operating by 1973 but was delayed due to the oil crisis. From a position in Harold Wilson's Labour cabinet, George Thomson was appointed as European Commissioner for Regional Policy. While the UK government effectively blocked the German proposal for a common social policy, the ERDF was established in 1975 under considerable pressure from the UK and Italy, signalling the UK's ability and political will to influence the direction of European social policy both negatively and positively.

Responsibility for the direction of the Commission's various activities is distributed between member states. When the UK joined the EC, it was assigned the social affairs portfolio, while the French and Germans held the more commanding financial portfolios. As Director-General for Social Affairs (1973–76), Michael Shanks, a UK economist, played a lead role in delivering the Commission's first social action programme.

Shanks (1977: vii) presaged that it would be essential for the EC to develop 'a viable social policy that is seen to relate to the problems and priorities confronting the man and woman in the street, and in which the relative roles of the Community and the individual member-States [sic] are clearly defined'. In line with the founding members' conception of social policy, the programme focussed primarily on employment and working conditions, and the relationship between management and labour. In a speech before an audience in the UK, Shanks (1973: 2) sought to justify the programme by highlighting the need to extend the benefits of economic growth to less privileged sectors of the population, including migrant workers, depicted as 'a kind of depressed sub-proletariat'. He also stressed the importance of dealing with the effects of environmental pollution on the quality of life. Shanks (1977: 9) described economic growth and an active social policy not only as compatible but also as mutually dependent if the Community was to improve its 'human face'. His assessment of the relationship between the economic and social dimensions would later justify a broader proactive approach to social policy.

Hywel Ceri Jones, recognised as one of seven prominent 'policy entrepreneurs' in EU education policy (Corbett, 2005: 17), also began working at the Commission in 1973. Jones was appointed as head of division for Education and Youth Policies within the Directorate-General (DG) for Research, Science and Education. Unlike Shanks and many of his contemporaries, Jones remained at the Commission for 25 years. He worked with several UK Commissioners in developing education as an area of social policy not specified in the EEC Treaty, and which many member states, including the UK, did not consider to lie within EU competence. While president of the Commission (1976–81), Roy Jenkins was instrumental in transferring Jones' directorate to the DG for Social Affairs, thereby formally recognising education as a legitimate area of EC social policy.

Under the EEC Treaty (article 157 §2), members of the Commission were required to perform their duties 'with complete independence' from national governments. In practice, as political appointees, Commissioners exercise their discretion to promote or defend national interests (Killermann, 2016) or, as shown in this chapter, to advance policies that may conflict with, or contest, those being pursued by their national leaders. As a pro-marketeer and advocate of political union, Jenkins had resigned from the Labour Party when he found himself at odds with its leadership in 1972 over EC membership. He did not intend to use his position in Brussels to support UK government interests (Jenkins, 1989: 546). Rather, he decided to promote monetary union as the flagship policy by which he would be remembered. Among his arguments was that it would stimulate employment and even out regional differences. He gave assurances that monetary union would not create a need for social or welfare spending to be centralised (Campbell, 2014: 3). Significantly, all the heads of state or government, except the UK's Labour Prime Minister, James Callaghan, adopted Jenkins' proposal.

Balancing the social and economic dimensions

Jenkins found himself in a difficult position when the UK (Conservative) government was seeking to renegotiate its contribution to the EU budget under Prime Minister Margaret Thatcher. By 1980, the UK was due to become the largest net contributor to the EC's budget (George, 1998: 132–3). The government's preoccupation in the early 1980s with the budget and a price-fixing package for the Common Agricultural Policy revealed the limits of any shared approach that might have existed concerning the role of social policy in economic integration. Thatcher's stance on the issue established the UK's adversarial reputation within the EC, reminiscent of President de Gaulle's 'empty chair' tactics in the 1960s (Guyomarch, Machin and Ritchie, 1998: 144).

After Jenkins' departure from Brussels, between 1981 and 1985, Jones worked with Ivor Richard, another former Labour member of parliament, who had been appointed as Commissioner for Employment, Social Affairs, Education and Training. Richard supported Jones in developing the successful drive for the Erasmus Decision 1987, as well as in extending the reach of the ESF (Corbett, 2005: 108–11, 154). Richard also provided strong support for the Commission's first equal opportunities action programme (1982–86) (Hoskyns, 1996: 146).

While the UK government's attention was diverted away from social affairs by economic concerns, the Commission seized the opportunity to bring forward its own social agenda. In the preamble to a Solemn Declaration on European Union in 1983, all the heads of state or government resolved 'to accord a high proority [sic] to the Community's social progress and in particular to the problem of employment by the development of a European social policy' (Preamble). They reiterated and amplified the objective signalled in the EEC Treaty for 'effective action in the social field to alleviate unemployment ... at both Community and national levels in particular by means of specific action on behalf of young people' (§3.1.1). Because her overarching objective was the completion of the single European market with the UK as the principal mover, despite her strong reservations about the Commission's encroachment into the social domain, Thatcher signed up to the Declaration.

In a context where the UK government was actively supporting the single market agenda, Jacques Delors as President of the European Commission (1985–95) entrusted Francis Cockfield, the UK Commissioner (appointed by Thatcher) for Internal Market, Customs Union and Taxation, and vice-president of the Commission (1984–88), with the major task of designing, drafting and implementing the 1986 Single European Act (SEA) as the first in a long series of treaty reforms. Cockfield (1994: 48) and Delors exploited the opportunity to deliver action in the regional and social field 'in parallel with progress on the Internal Market'.

While the SEA was being negotiated, the UK government appeared to have understood the benefits of displaying willingness to compromise over its vision of the relationship between social and economic policy. The government was put to the test, however, in 1986 when the UK assumed the rotating presidency of the European Council. During the run-up to the SEA, the French had continued to make the case for employment, dialogue between management and labour, and cooperation and consultation over social protection arrangements. For Delors (1985: xviii), social policy in these terms was necessary to deepen the common market. The positioning of the social dimension in relation to the internal market, alongside questions of institutional reform and the role of redistributive funds, remained fundamental points of disagreement with the UK government, which put forward its own plan to tackle unemployment by freeing the market. The UK plan was rejected on grounds that it did not go far enough, whereas the final package agreed by the EC's employment ministers went beyond what the UK was willing to accept (George, 1998: 187–9).

The Commission was treaty-bound to consult the European Economic and Social Committee (EESC) (EEC Treaty, article 198), on which UK workers' and employers' organisations and other interest groups were well represented (Westlake, 2016). While preparations were being made for Economic and Monetary Union (EMU) to be institutionalised in the next stage after the SEA, Delors asked the EESC to engage in a general discussion on the possible content of a Community Charter of Fundamental Rights of Workers as part of his wider project for a social dimension in the Maastricht Treaty.

The EESC's opinion, issued in 1987, 'defined the foundations of a social Europe. It insisted on the effective assurance of social rights in the Community legal order, a social dimension to the internal market, and a Community-level social dialogue' (Westlake, 2016:

151). The preamble to the 1989 Charter defined the parameters for the relationship between the social and economic dimensions of the EU, stating that 'in the context of the establishment of the single European market, the same importance must be attached to the social aspects as to the economic aspects and ..., therefore, they must be developed in a balanced manner'.

An address by Delors to the UK's Trades Union Congress (TUC) in 1988, shortly before the Community Charter was adopted (without the UK), confirmed the meaning that Delors attributed to the social dimension, and provoked Thatcher into making her controversial Bruges speech. In his address, Delors (1988: 3) reiterated his understanding of the social dimension as a 'vital element' in the internal market, referring to a 'uniquely European model of society', based on guaranteed social rights, social solidarity, protection of the weakest and collective bargaining, to be preserved and enhanced in the face of the threat from globalisation and the massive unemployment that it entailed. Delors' emphasis on the primacy of cooperation in managing diversity, while preserving identities and cultures, encouraged a more pro-European stance on the Left in the UK, hitherto opposed to European integration (Jenkins, 2010; Powell, 2018: 140–1).

The UK's ambivalent relationship with the social dimension

The UK government had always accepted that the project to free the EC's internal market must be accompanied by minimum EC-wide standards on health and safety at work on grounds that, otherwise, employers might try to achieve a competitive advantage by reducing safety standards (George, 1998: 240). Although she made no explicit reference to social policy development in her 1998 Bruges speech, Thatcher strongly rejected the introduction of any 'new regulations which raise the cost of employment and make Europe's labour market less flexible and less competitive with overseas suppliers'. The UK government opposed EC legislative proposals on working hours and employees' rights, at that time with support from the Confederation of British Industry (George, 1998: 241).

When John Major succeeded Thatcher as Prime Minister in 1990, he endorsed her restrained approach to the social dimension and blocked the incorporation of the Community Charter in the body of the 1992 Maastricht Treaty. The Agreement on Social Policy (referred to as the Social Chapter) was relegated to a protocol, which did not have force of law and left decisions on implementation procedures to individual member states.

The social dimension continued to be the main substantive point of disagreement between the New Labour government and the Conservative opposition in 1997, whereas they were united in their hostility to the single currency. Like Thatcher, Tony Blair (2006) as leader of the Labour Party wanted the UK to work in partnership with other independent sovereign states to build a successful European Community. While Thatcher had been intent on blocking social initiatives using the UK's veto, when he became prime minister, Blair sought to advance a positive social agenda, particularly in the field of employment, based on his conception of security and flexibility (Wall, 2008: 162, 165–6, 214).

Blair adopted a more constructive approach using the Social Chapter to bring about change across Europe, with a view to enabling UK citizens to enjoy the same social rights as their European neighbours. Rather than using the European Employment Strategy (EES), launched in 1997, to legitimise their own reform agenda, Blair and his successor Gordon Brown sought to 'upload' Labour's flexibility and welfare-to-work policies to EU level (Hopkin and Van Wijnbergen, 2011: 275).

When David Cameron led the Conservative Party back to power in 2010 – until 2015 in coalition with the Liberal Democrats –his main concern was with economic and political issues as he strived to restore party unity over Europe (Cameron, 2013). He quickly became aware that 'the distributional impacts and the actual and perceived pressures on access to local public services and housing at a time of austerity ... [were] the political issue which electrified the Conservative Party and UKIP, but also the Labour heartlands, many of which were to vote heavily for Brexit' (Rogers, 2018: 254). In relation to other member states, however, the economic situation in the UK was considered 'healthy', which weakened Cameron's case for special treatment to be granted to the UK.

Protecting sovereignty and the national interest

Jean Monnet's plan for European postwar reconstruction in the coal and steel industries required member states to accept the principle of a supranational authority with its own financial resources. The French were reluctant to surrender their sovereignty over economic decision making, and the model was not adopted for the EEC. This section examines how, as the EEC Treaty's social provisions were progressively supplemented and implemented, the relationship between supranationalism and national sovereignty intensified conflicts between the UK government and EU institutions, especially the Commission and the CJEU. It shows how the UK sought to safeguard national control in the social domain, and considers how plans to harmonise social provisions gave way to measures designed to promote coordination and cooperation.

The implications of EEC social law for national sovereignty

When, with Denmark and Ireland, the UK's application to join the EC was accepted, by approving the European Communities Act 1972, the UK parliament agreed to give EC law supremacy over national law, including any social legislation previously passed. Under the Act, parliament wrote into national law all the treaty commitments – *acquis communautaire* – that it had had no hand in determining or shaping. The UK thus signed up to principles that would, in later years, be perceived to threaten the nation's sovereignty in the social domain, as views about the national interest evolved and polarised under pressure from public and parliamentary opinion, not least due to the personalities, beliefs, judgements and prejudices of politicians and, especially, prime ministers (Wall, 2013: 2; Adonis, 2018: xii).

Sovereignty is closely associated with perceptions of the national interest. Like other member states, UK governments were prepared to support policies that were in line with the national interest and to block progress when they felt their sovereignty was threatened. In 1973, all the partners were being 'awkward' when defending their national interests, but the UK had yet to learn how to play 'the Community game in such a way as to appear to be *communautaire*' (George, 1998: 70). Notwithstanding differences between UK political parties in their conceptions of social policy, over the years of EC/EU membership, governments of Right and Left were unwilling to relinquish sovereignty over their national social protection systems.

When Prime Minister Edward Heath took the UK into the EU, he recognised the importance of 'pooling sovereignty' to mutual advantage (McManus, 2018: 98). By contrast, in his party's 1974 election manifesto, Harold Wilson, as Labour leader, saw no role for the EC in dealing with domestic issues. He spelled out Labour's broad understanding of social policy to mean: shifting the balance of power and wealth in favour of working people and their families; eliminating poverty both at home and abroad; making power in industry genuinely accountable to workers; achieving greater economic equality of income, wealth and living standards, and greater social equality through full employment, housing, education and social benefits; and improving the environment in which people live and work and spend their leisure. Labour strongly criticised what they considered as the 'draconian curtailment of the power of the British Parliament [under the previous Conservative government] to settle questions affecting vital British interests' (Wilson, 1974).

The concept of a unified or federal Europe was alien to the UK government, who saw it as challenging the supremacy of the nation state. For Thatcher, the growing powers of EU institutions came to represent a totally unacceptable threat to national sovereignty, not least in the social area. In 1985, the UK government demonstrated its refusal to relinquish national sovereignty by retaining control over its national borders when Belgium, France, Germany, Luxembourg and the Netherlands signed the Schengen Agreement.

Although Thatcher was 'not keen on Community action' in the social and employment fields, she was prepared to accept the inclusion of references, both in the Solemn Declaration and in the SEA 1986, to European 'union', but only because she understood it to be an evolving long-term process rather than an immediate goal (Wall, 2008: 23). In a pamphlet circulated to the other heads of state or government in 1984, she set out practical guidelines for achieving what she meant by 'union'. The references she made to social issues, as defined in the EEC Treaty, concerned the need for policies guaranteeing 'the relevance of the Community to the problems, particularly unemployment, which affect our societies' and that 'will improve the quality as well as the standard of life in the Community' (British Prime Minister, 1984: 81).

In a much quoted statement from her Bruges speech, Thatcher (1988) declared: 'We have not successfully rolled back the frontiers of the state in Britain, only to see them re-imposed at a European level with a European super-state exercising a new dominance from Brussels.' She went on to assert: 'Certainly we want to see Europe more united and with a greater sense of common purpose. But it must be in a way which preserves the different traditions, parliamentary powers and sense of national pride in one's own country'. Few national leaders, then or later, would dispute these claims.

Treaty change and national sovereignty

A major source of contention for the Conservative government in the 1980s was Cockfield's proposal in the SEA (article 21) to extend qualified majority voting (QMV) to a larger number of areas, including social policy, to standardise VAT rates between countries, and to expand the powers of the European Parliament. Denmark and Greece shared the UK's objections to any weakening of national sovereignty through QMV and the extension of the European Parliament's powers. Thatcher could not accept what she saw as Cockfield's 'disloyalty', over the QMV issue, and he was not re-appointed for a second term in Brussels (George, 1998: 152, 197). Although the Council eventually agreed to retain unanimity for social security and social protection, QMV was introduced in the SEA for health and safety measures, and was written into subsequent treaties. At the time, Thatcher may not have appreciated fully how the extension of QMV could be used to expand the EU's social policy competence through binding social legislation that pushed the boundaries of interpretation into areas that were 'legally and politically controversial' (Wall, 2008: 209).

As Thatcher's successor when she was forced out of office in 1990, John Major attempted to broker a compromise within the divided Conservative Party, while also averting the threat of new regulatory burdens on industry in the UK by negotiating an opt-out from the Social Chapter. At the same time, the government opted out from the eurozone, thereby removing itself from the negotiating table when many issues involving sovereignty over social affairs were being discussed.

The change to a Labour government in 1997 brought a shift in approach to European social affairs. Having signed up to the Social Chapter, Prime Minister Blair was open to some modest increases in QMV, except for tax, social security and foreign policy, where sovereignty remained paramount (Wall, 2008: 214). Both he and his chancellor, Gordon Brown, did not rule out that the UK would join the euro if and when the necessary conditions were met.

The Coalition Agreement of 2010 between the Conservative and Liberal Democrats stated unambiguously that the UK government would prevent any further transfer of sovereignty or powers during their mandate (House of Lords European Union Committee, 2015: 5). In presenting his vision of the EU for a domestic audience and echoing his predecessors, in his 2013 Bloomberg speech, Cameron stressed the central importance of protecting national interests and of defending sovereignty as a defining characteristic of the UK as an island state.

From harmonisation to cooperation

UK governments had consistently been in favour of enlargement, which was seen as a priority when the UK held the rotating presidency of the EC for the first time in 1977. They expected enlargement to dilute and hamper European integration by making bureaucratisation, centralisation and harmonisation of social policy more difficult to achieve (George, 1998: 126).

A certain amount of diluted harmonisation was, however, acceptable to the UK in the field of education and training. In 1998 the French, German, Italian and UK ministers for education signed a joint declaration on harmonisation of the architecture of the European higher education system, thereby launching the Bologna Process (Allègre et al, 1998). They unambiguously argued for a new form of flexible European coordination to be 'implemented at national level within the existing structures of higher education–government relations', but without the signatories ceding control over their institutions to the EU (Corbett, 2003: 2). The proposal particularly suited Germany as it safeguarded devolved control over higher education by the *Länder*.

The UK also signed up to the Copenhagen Process for action in the field of vocational training, which was initiated in 2002 at the Barcelona summit along similar lines to the Bologna declaration for higher education. Again, the aim was not to harmonise systems but through cooperation to develop common European references and principles regarding quality, transparency and recognition, as well as flexible and more individualised pathways to enhance progression.

Successive UK governments endorsed a similar approach in other areas of social policy. For example, in his Bloomberg speech,

Cameron (2013) stressed the need to avoid one-size-fits-all policies and to espouse a flexible approach based not on harmonisation but on cooperation. 'This vision [he later argued in his 2015 Chatham House speech] … is not the same as those who want to build an ever closer political union – but it is just as valid'.

The UK's influence on the distribution of competences

The UK government was not alone in seeking to protect national sovereignty and interests from European integration and harmonisation of national social welfare systems. Successive governments in the UK in alliances with other member states continually sought to prevent EU institutions from extending their competence over social affairs. This section considers how the UK influenced the distribution of competences between EU institutions and member states in the social domain by pushing for implementation of the subsidiarity principle, by blocking unpalatable proposals at intergovernmental conferences or by obtaining opt-outs from social programmes and legislation, while Commission officials and advisers from the UK worked together to bring forward far-reaching social policy proposals.

Safeguarding national competences

There is evidence to suggest that, already in the 1970s, 'British influence and hesitation' on both sides of the political spectrum were having an impact on Community thinking about its role in shaping social policy (Wall, 2008: 3). Heads of state or government were demonstrating that they shared a deep-seated reluctance to adopt binding social legislation. Council Resolution of 21 January 1974 concerning a social action programme provided a clear statement of the Council's conception at that time of the measured role the Commission should play as a social policy actor. In keeping with the terms of the EEC Treaty as understood by the UK, the aim was not to seek standard solutions or transfer to EEC level responsibilities that could best be assumed at national level.

Supported by other member states, the UK argued successfully for the adoption of the principle of subsidiarity, prefigured in the 1974 Resolution. The subsidiarity principle later became firmly embedded in EU treaties (Treaty of Lisbon, article 5 §3) and was to serve as a recurring theme in policy documents mapping and laying down the EU's social policy competence in an ever-enlarging and culturally more diverse Community.

Four months after the signing of the Maastricht Treaty in February 1992, and the UK's opt-out from the Social Chapter, Norman Lamont, then UK Chancellor of the Exchequer under Major, appended his signature to a non-binding recommendation from the Council on the convergence of social protection objectives and policies, but not of national social systems. The Recommendation (92/442/EEC) clarified the EU's formal consensual position on social policy by defining the limits to EU-level social policy competence. It recognised that differences in social security cover might act as a serious brake on the free movement of workers and exacerbate regional imbalances, particularly between the north and south of the Community (Greece, Portugal and Spain having joined the EU). In line with the UK's stance, point 25 affirmed that, 'because of the diversity of the schemes and their roots in national cultures, it is for Member States to determine how their social protection schemes should be framed and the arrangements for financing and organizing them'.

Through soft law alternatives to fundamental rights

During the 1990s, the Commission added what was intended to be a less controversial instrument – the open method of coordination (OMC) - to the EU's arsenal in the social field, indicating that it was seeking to circumvent confrontation with hostile member states such as the UK. OMC was first applied in the 1998 Employment Guidelines to add value at EU level when little scope existed for legislative solutions. For the UK government, OMC afforded a welcome alternative to hard law in the social policy field since it left detailed policy implementation to member states.

The Amsterdam, Nice and Lisbon Treaties (signed in 1997, 2000 and 2007, respectively) legitimised the expansion of the Commission's competence in the social domain. OMC helped prepare the way for the launch of the Charter of Fundamental Rights of the European Union (2000/C 364/01), which was subsequently incorporated into the Lisbon Treaty. The new Charter differed from the 1989 Community Charter in that it guaranteed all rights, not just social, for all citizens, not just workers. The 2000 Charter irrevocably extended the boundaries of EU social policy beyond the workplace to the reconciliation of family and professional life, the protection and care of children and older people, social and housing assistance, preventive health care, and religious belief and practice. The Charter was an official document agreed by all member states. Although the UK did not request an opt-out, with Poland it negotiated a clarifying protocol, which was annexed to the consolidated version of the Treaty on the Functioning of the European Union (TFEU, Protocol 30 article 1) when it came into force in 2010. The protocol meant that the two governments were not bound by rulings of the CJEU that might be incompatible with those of their national courts.

By 2006, a streamlined version of the OMC had been extended from employment to social protection systems, social ex/inclusion, education, research, immigration, pensions, health and long-term care. These were almost all areas where the Commission had already initiated policy programmes at national or local levels, supported by UK social scientists.

Building EU social policy capacity and the evidence base

While UK governments were resisting treaty reform, loss of sovereignty and the expanding competence of the European Commission, UK appointees as commissioners, directors-general, advisers or coordinators of projects and networks were helping shape the social policy agenda. This section examines how UK social scientists contributed to the Commission's evidence base on the social situation in the EU through their studies, reports and capacity-building activities in the social domain.

Monitoring and reporting social developments

Article 122 of the EEC Treaty required the Commission to report annually to the Council, including 'a special chapter on the development of the social situation within the Community'. Article 1 of the Social Chapter in the 1992 Maastricht Treaty set out the social objectives to which the EU remained committed: 'the promotion of employment, improved living and working conditions, proper social protection, dialogue between management and labour, the development of human resources with a view to lasting high employment and the combating of exclusion'. Article 7 specified that the Commission should report annually to Council, the European Parliament and EESC on the demographic situation in the Community with a view to achieving the objectives in article 1.

In compiling its reports and in taking forward its social action programmes, the Commission relied heavily on independent social policy experts to coordinate the monitoring and evaluation of the many European agencies, networks and observatories, which were set up with the Council's agreement. Stephen Wall (2008: 218), a former diplomat and close observer of the European scene, has argued that 'Britain, within the limitations of its constitutional view, has been a European pioneer in its advocacy of reform'. The same could be said for its input in the social domain. By helping to create an evidence base to inform policy, UK social scientists can be seen to have made a significant contribution to policy development. They assisted the Commission in preparing and delivering action programmes in several social policy areas, and in its monitoring and reporting activities. Working closely with colleagues in other member states, they also played an advocacy role, exemplified in the area of gender equality (Hoskyns, 1996).

UK influence on the reach of social policy

From the mid-1980s, the Council and the Commission received reports on the demographic situation from the EESC. In 1994, the Commission compiled its own annual demographic report, assisted in the planning stages by a group of 16 scientific experts, four of whom were from the UK, more than from any other member state. The reports were designed: to identify and raise questions of importance for demographic trends; and to describe and analyse demographic trends and their impacts on policies under the aegis of the then DG for Employment, Industrial Relations and Social Affairs.

Although only the European Medicines Agency and European Banking Authority were based in London, UK social scientists maintained a strong presence in other European agencies, often in leadership positions, most notably in the European Foundation for the Improvement of Living and Working Conditions (Eurofound) in Dublin, which was centrally concerned with the issues identified in the Social Chapter.

From the late 1970s through to 1999, Graham Room (1983), a UK academic, acted as consultant and coordinator for the Commission in the development of its social action programmes in the field of poverty and social exclusion. The UK coordinating team played a major role in developing procedures for evaluating the Commission's actions and projects, and for raising awareness of the political implication of comparing the performance of different countries. They demonstrated, for example, how drawing a poverty line, could be 'a highly political act' (Brown, 1987: 49). When, in support of the development of the social dimension, the Lisbon summit in March 2000 formally applied the OMC in the area of poverty and social exclusion, Anthony Atkinson (2000), an internationally reputed UK economist and researcher on inequality and poverty studies, made a proposal, which the Commission actively pursued, for benchmarking poverty measures as a first step towards a European social inclusion agenda. By identifying national competences, he gave member states the opportunity to learn from the best performers in the EU.

When the UK joined the EC in 1973, the ground had been prepared, particularly by prominent Belgian and French women, for a spate of activity in the area of gender equality resulting in a series of ground-breaking directives. The UK seconded large numbers of national experts to the Commission's Equal Opportunities Unit. By the 1990s, over half the coordinators on the Commission's third medium-term Community action programme on equal opportunities for women and men (1991–95) were from the UK (Stratigaki, 2000: 47). Jill Rubery (1996), also a UK academic, coordinated the European Network of Experts on the Situation of Women in the Labour Market during the same period. Like the other networks and observatories, their task was primarily to collect and analyse data about trends and patterns within member states. They also provided a comparative synthesis for the Commission to use in its reports and policy proposals. Their remit extended to lobbying as they successfully argued the case for gender mainstreaming.

From the 1980s, the Commission was already developing European competence in areas that were prime examples of the subsidiarity principle, especially in the UK. In 1989, the Commission formally established a network of 12 independent national experts, known as the European Observatory on National Family Policies, coordinated by a UK team between 1994 (the International Year of the Family) and 1997. Rather than simply profiling each country's activities in the area, the UK coordinators developed comparisons of issues such as family incomes and tax-benefit policies (Ditch, Barnes and Bradshaw, 1996). They assembled evidence of how the costs of raising children were shared between families and the state in different countries, thereby challenging any prospect of formal competence sharing with EU institutions.

Other UK social scientists made a contribution to the EU's social policy evidence base between 1986 and 1996 in a related area through the Commission's Network on Childcare and other Measures to Reconcile Employment and Family Responsibilities. The UK coordinator of the Network, Peter Moss (1994), and his international team developed a strong focus on leave arrangements for workers with children. They provided a robust source of data to inform the Council Recommendation on child care (92/241/EEC), the Communication from the Commission: Towards an EU Strategy on the Rights of the Child (COM(2006)367 final), and the Work–life Balance Directive (2010/18/EU).

As concern with the impact of population ageing moved onto the agenda, the Commission established an Observatory on Ageing and Older People in 1990, led by Alan Walker, a UK social scientist with a distinguished track record for research into ageing. His efforts were to be concentrated on four areas: living standards and way of life; employment and the labour market; health and social care; and the social integration of older people in both formal and informal settings (Walker, Guillemard and Alber, 1993). These tasks complemented the work of Eurofound and other observatories and networks. When, in 2012, the Commission and the United Nations Economic Commission for Europe jointly funded the Active Ageing Index project, it was coordinated by another UK academic, Asghar Zaidi (2015).

The European Observatory on Health Systems and Policies, established in 1998, created two research hubs in London, hosted by the Department of Health Policy at the London School of Economics, and the Centre for Global Chronic Conditions at the London School of Hygiene and Tropical Medicine. The Observatory's mission was 'to support and promote evidence-based health policy-making through comprehensive and rigorous analysis of the dynamics of health-care systems in Europe'. It served as a clearing house on health care reforms, charged with agreeing on a set of common, fundamental principles that should underlie reforms of health systems.

Supporting links between social science and policy

In the early 2000s, the Commission was called upon to demonstrate value for money and the relevance to policy of EU-funded research under the framework programmes (FPs), particularly in the social sciences. The Commission invited researchers and consultants from across the EU to prepare policy reviews synthesising the findings from social science projects on policy issues and research directions. Of the 20 policy reviews commissioned by the DG for Research in 2006, 10 were drafted by UK social scientists.

When the Commission grouped together the different networks under the European Observatory on Demography and the Social Situation in 2005, social scientists from the UK were again well represented as coordinators. They also served as advisers on bodies such as the High Level Group of Experts on Demographic Issues. Their brief included acting as contributors and reviewers for the annual demographic reports, which focussed increasingly on the relationship between research and policy and the implementation of evidence-based policy.

The pre-eminence of UK social scientists and their contribution to social policy development was further demonstrated by the fact that UK social science research became one of the few areas where the UK was a net beneficiary of EU funds. During the life of the framework programmes, UK social sciences outperformed both other disciplines in the UK and social scientists elsewhere in the EU by attracting disproportionately high levels of EU research funding (Hantrais and Thomas Lenihan, 2016). The European Social Survey, initiated by Roger Jowell at the National Centre for Social Research in London, obtained FP5 funding in 2000. It was awarded the Descartes Prize in 2005 for 'excellence in collaborative scientific research', and became one of the first research infrastructures to be awarded European Research Infrastructure Consortium (ERIC) status in 2013.

Assessing UK influence on social policy in the EU

During the 45 years of its EU membership, the UK was not alone in contesting the place of the social dimension in European policymaking, or in seeking to prevent the loss of control over its social institutions. UK governments were prepared to play a lead role in accommodating a multi-scalar and flexible social Europe and in preferring soft to hard law in the social field. Arguably, in their efforts to protect national sovereignty and preserve national interests, they positioned themselves outside the core through their opt-outs and blocking tactics, thereby inadvertently restraining their ability to shape social policy, as well as the impact of EU social legislation on the UK.

In light of the examples cited in this chapter, the otherwise predominantly negative impression provided in the international media and party-political pronouncements of the adversarial relationship between the UK and its European partners needs to be revisited with reference to the social domain. Through their advisory roles and participation in EU-level committees, research projects and networks, UK nationals employed by the Commission and UK social scientists undoubtedly played a more constructive role. They contributed to the advancement and sharing of knowledge, evidence-based policy, cross-border learning and policy transfer. Bypassing bureaucratic constraints, they contributed a more positive influence on European social policy, which has been largely neglected by critics of the relationship between the UK and the EU in the social domain.

FOUR

Brexit and UK social policy

Political scientists (Evans and Menon, 2017: xiii) have argued that: 'The Referendum, and the events that have followed it, can only be understood via a grasp both of the UK's relationship with the EU and of more general developments in British politics over the last few decades.' The review in this book of the events leading up to the signing of the Treaty establishing the European Economic Community (EEC) in 1957 and its implementation would suggest that, in the social domain, a much longer time span is necessary to uncover the origins of the many factors explaining the Leave vote in the 2016 referendum. The Leave and Remain campaigns highlighted to differing degrees the loss of control over national social welfare systems and the encroachment of the European Commission and Court of Justice of the European Union (CJEU) in other areas of social policy. They both emphasised the threat posed to member states by migration. All of these issues can be traced back to the EEC Treaty.

The UK's membership of the European Communities/European Union (EC/EU) coincided with a period during which the notion of social Europe, or European social integration, progressively moved onto the agenda based on a broad set of shared social values, standards and objectives (Vandenbroucke, Barnard and De Baere, 2017: xix). By the time the UK triggered article 50 on 29 March 2017, EU soft and hard law spanned the whole panoply of social rights, enshrined in the 2000 Charter of Fundamental Rights of the European Union. The longstanding hostility of UK governments to EU intervention in national social affairs was reflected in public opinion. The level of contestation of European authority became more acute in the wake of the 2008 global financial and 2010 eurozone crises, as did open expressions of euroscepticism and disaffection with the European project among political parties and electorates across the EU.

During more than 40 years of EC/EU membership, successive UK governments pledged to give the public an opportunity to determine what relationship the UK should have with the EU (Westlake, 2017). Until 2016, only the Labour government of 1974–76 had fulfilled their commitment to hold a referendum on continuing membership of the EC/EU. In 1975, just two years after joining, the electorate voted for the status quo. The situation was very different in 2016 after 43 years of membership: arguably voting patterns in the referendum were heavily influenced by the failure of both UK and EU institutions to solve enduring social problems (Barnard, 2017: 480–4).

In adopting the long view, this chapter considers the arguments contributing to an understanding of the meaning of Brexit for UK social policy by exploring:

- what role the social dimension played in the commitments of successive UK governments to hold referendums;
- how social policy became a central issue in the 2016 referendum campaign;
- what role the social dimension played in the outcome of the referendum and the withdrawal negotiations;
- how the UK's decision to leave the EU might impact on future social policy development in the UK.

The chapter provides further evidence of the importance of the recurring themes in the social domain that characterised the UK's membership of the EC/EU. They were present in the period leading up to the 2016 referendum, in the negotiations with the EU and in the UK government's 2017 and 2018 white papers and withdrawal agreement. The rejection of supranationalism and the efforts to protect national sovereignty over social affairs were expressed in claims to take back control from EU institutions. Associated issues about the distribution of competences between EU and national institutions were raised in proposals for a flexible partnership with the EU. Negotiations focussed on the need to continue to match social standards and ensure the status of former and future intra-European migrants in accessing social rights as and when the UK left the EU. Following the pattern established during the UK's EC/EU membership, the withdrawal negotiations demonstrated how the process of constant adaptation, consensus and compromise, characteristic of interstate relations, played out in the social policy domain.

Referendums and withdrawal on the agenda

Social policy has long been a contested area for EU member states, their governments and their populations, as illustrated throughout this book. Even before the UK joined the EC in 1973, its governments had questioned the benefits of membership, not least in the social domain. Substantial disagreement between Right and Left and within political parties was evident from the outset regarding the extent to which European institutions should develop social policy competence. As in other member states, the personalities and personal ambitions of national leaders, under pressures from domestic politics and interstate coalition building, played a critical role in determining negotiating positions and outcomes at meetings of the Council of Ministers, and in proposals to resort to the popular vote to support treaty reform. Arguably, every UK government since 1973 has needed to 'watch its back on

Europe' (Wall, 2008: 217). A comment made when James Callaghan was leader of a Labour government in the late 1970s can be applied to the Brexit process: 'Domestic political constraints and international economic objectives came together to mould the positions taken up by the British Government on each of the European issues which arose during the period of Callaghan's premiership.' (George, 1998: 107) Conservative and Labour Party leaders, both in government and opposition, pledged to hold referendums on continuing EC/EU membership to unite their divided domestic audiences and political parties.

This section tracks the events illustrating the reluctance and hesitation of UK governments to commit fully to the goals of economic, political and, even more so, social union. It shows how politicians from all parties used the prospect of holding a referendum and/or the threat of withdrawal to canvass public support in managing the relationship with EU institutions as well as the divisions within their own ranks.

The 1975 UK referendum on continuing membership

Although UK politicians often proposed calling a referendum on European matters, unlike many other member states, the UK only once held a referendum on EU issues. The unwillingness of UK governments to use referendums can be attributed to 'the doctrine of absolute sovereignty of Parliament' (Westlake, 2017: 5); traditionally the UK parliamentary and electoral system gives the public adequate opportunity to express its opinion. Arguably, the UK did not hold referendums due to the fear that a negative vote would result in the prime minister being forced out of office if a referendum was used to obtain a vote of confidence.

The UK was reluctant to join the EEC when it was first proposed but was then prevented from joining on two occasions by French vetoes, respectively with a Conservative then a Labour government in power. The reasons for these inauspicious beginnings did not specifically concern social issues, and the UK government did not see fit to consult its people when the French electorate approved the accession of the applicant states in a referendum in 1972. The other three candidate countries, Denmark, Ireland and Norway, which applied to join at the same time as the UK, used referendums to ensure popular support for membership. Norway did not join then or later because its electorate voted against membership.

In 1975, the UK was to become the only member state to hold a referendum on continuing membership. Greenland, as an autonomous territory of Denmark, voted to leave the EC in 1982. After the introduction of home rule in 1979, fearing the loss of their fishing rights (their main source of livelihood) under the Common Fisheries Policy, Greenlanders began the process of leaving the EC. Their exit took place long before John Kerr (2017), a former UK ambassador to the EU, drafted article 50 stipulating the arrangements for leaving the Union. Following three years of tough formal negotiations, Greenland left the EC in 1985 and, today, has a partnership agreement with the EU (De la Baume, 2016).

Edward Heath, a Conservative pro-European integration prime minister, signed the UK's accession agreement in 1972, only to be replaced in a general election a year after UK membership took effect by Harold Wilson leading an anti-European Labour Party. During the February 1974 election campaign, Wilson announced his intention, if elected, to renegotiate the terms of membership, among others, explicitly to prevent further encroachment of EC institutions in national social affairs. If satisfactory terms could not be renegotiated, and if a referendum resulted in a vote to leave, his intention was to withdraw from the EC. He used the threat of withdrawal primarily to fend off domestic opposition, 'a relentlessly hostile Press' and a 'bitterly divided' party (Rosamond, 2007: 59; Wall, 2008: 210), as would his successors in later years. For the anti-marketeers in the Labour Party, backed by the block vote of the trades unions who did not consider that their interests were being served, sovereignty over social affairs was a decisive issue and was not negotiable. Wilson sought to stand back from the 1975 referendum campaign (Ashcroft and Oakeshott, 2016: 565). Then, as in 2016, there appeared to be 'little prospect of holding the cabinet to the principle of collective responsibility' (George, 1998: 91). He therefore left individual members free to dissent from the party line in public. Meanwhile, as leader of the opposition, Margaret Thatcher (1975) campaigned strongly for a vote to keep Britain in Europe on grounds of her support for the common market.

In 1975, the UK held what was to be its first nationwide referendum on Europe (Dinan, 2007: 159). The principle was thus acknowledged that a referendum could be held and that 'the longstanding eschewal of direct democracy was no more' (Westlake, 2017: 6). The electorate was asked: 'Do you think the United Kingdom should stay in the European Community (the Common Market)?' Although the result was a landslide decision to remain (67.2% to 32.8%, turnout 64%), the popular vote was deemed to be 'unenthusiastic' and was interpreted as 'a vote for the *status quo*' (Butler and Kitzinger, 1976: 279–80). However, a concordance between the majority of the people and the majority in parliament was achieved, so that: 'When the referendum was over, the issue ceased to divide the country.' The fact of having held a referendum established the legitimacy of Europe as 'an issue for parliamentary rebellion' (Westlake, 2017: 6).

Having secured the support of the people, Wilson made clear that, as members of the EEC, 'insofar as we press for interests of importance [this refers to issues of national importance which might be subject to a veto procedure in the institutions] we shall be doing no more and no less than our EEC partners' (Segal, 1975). The Wilson government then proceeded to attempt to block proposals for social legislation, for example on limiting lorry drivers' hours, arguing that it would destroy the UK's competitive advantage. Other EC member states interpreted his approach as 'a lack of Community spirit' (George, 1998: 98), an impression confirmed by the actions of subsequent UK prime ministers.

Avoiding referendums on Europe

Thatcher's adversarial stance over the European budget as prime minister, and her demand for reform of the Common Agricultural Policy in 1982, led President François Mitterrand and his Foreign Minister Claude Cheysson to suggest that it might be better for all concerned if the UK ceased to be a full member of the EC (George, 1998: 150). Thatcher's response to a question in parliament about UK membership was: 'We intend to remain full members of the EEC' (Prime Minister, 1982). Meanwhile, pursuing opposition to the EC, in their 1983 election manifesto under their leader Michael Foot, Labour pledged to begin negotiations to withdraw from the EU 'within the lifetime' of the following parliament. This threat did not materialise since Labour lost the election, and Thatcher began her second term in office.

Denmark and Ireland held referendums in 1987 on the terms of the Single European Act (SEA) 1986. The UK's Conservative government had accepted the extension of qualified majority voting (QMV) in the SEA to areas of social policy concerning health and safety, as a trade-off in return for the completion of the common market. Despite Labour's vote against, the UK parliament ratified the SEA, without putting it to the people.

When Neil Kinnock was leader of the Labour Party and of the opposition between 1983 and 1992, divisions within and between the political parties crystallised over the Commission's proposal for developing social policy. Labour had been in favour of the 1989 Community Charter, but voted against the 1992 Maastricht Treaty on European Union (Wall, 2008: 161, 217).

Italy held a referendum on the Maastricht Treaty in 1989, as did Denmark, France and Ireland in 1993. The Danish people rejected the Treaty, signalling growing public remoteness from the EU. A second referendum was needed in Denmark to obtain a 'Yes' vote after negotiating four opt-outs, including on Economic and Monetary Union (EMU). Had the negotiations not been successful, the Danes had announced their intention to leave (Wall, 2008:

139). The convergence criteria for EMU, which were also being negotiated in Maastricht, meant that governments would have to improve their public finances, often at the cost of their welfare programmes (Dinan, 2007: 163). The UK joined Denmark in refusing to sign up to EMU.

Rather than putting these questions to a referendum, on grounds that a parliament elected by the people should be responsible for ratification, the UK government exercised its prerogative by refusing to accept the terms of the Community Charter of the Fundamental Social Rights of Workers, which was to be incorporated in the Maastricht Treaty as its social dimension. When the Treaty was being finalised, John Major (Prime Minister, 1992) justified his decision to opt out of the Social Chapter. He argued before parliament that: 'Signing the social chapter would have removed from employers and employees in this country their right to determine for themselves such matters as working conditions.'

Mounting pressure for a UK referendum on Europe

In 1996, the businessman Sir James Goldsmith launched the Referendum Party to campaign for a people's vote on the UK's membership of the EU in the expectation that the result would be a decision to leave. Although his party secured only 3.5% of the vote at the 1997 general election, the result gave an indication of embryonic popular interest in the possibility of the UK at some point leaving the EU.

In their 1997 election manifesto, Labour announced that, if they held a referendum on Europe, a 'Yes' vote would be a 'pre-condition' for the UK to join the single currency. Referendums were called in Denmark and Ireland, but not the UK, to endorse the Amsterdam (1998) and Nice (2001) Treaties. After first voting 'No' in the referendum on Nice, Ireland negotiated concessions on defence and an enhanced role for its national parliament before holding a second referendum resulting in 62.9% in favour.

Tony Blair then committed the UK government to calling a referendum to ratify the EU's Constitutional Treaty when it was signed in 2004. Announcing his full support for a referendum, Blair claimed that it would protect the national veto on sensitive issues such as tax, social policy, defence and foreign policy. Labour, the Conservatives and Liberal Democrats all promised a referendum in their 2005 general election manifestos. By rejecting the Constitutional Treaty in referendums on ratification in 2005, France and the Netherlands signalled popular concern about the direction in which the EU was developing (Dinan, 2007: 164). Luxembourg and Spain held referendums, with positive outcomes, particularly in Spain (81.8% in favour). Six member states, including Denmark and the UK, cancelled plans to hold referendums when the French and Dutch results were announced.

In 2007, the Constitutional Treaty was replaced by the Lisbon Treaty, which embodied the 2000 Charter of Fundamental Rights of the European Union, albeit with a clarifying protocol for the UK and Poland. Again, the Irish government needed a second referendum before ratifying the Treaty. Again, it negotiated concessions to safeguard Irish sovereignty and to protect against any attempts by EU institutions to take control of its regulatory powers. It cited critical social issues such as the legalisation of abortion, which the Irish government wanted to resolve without intervention from the EU. Calls for a referendum in the UK once more went unanswered, allowing Blair to avoid having to fulfil his commitment to a people's vote on Europe for the duration of his premiership.

David Cameron had long considered Europe to be a toxic subject. When he became leader of the Conservative Party in 2007, he gave a 'cast-iron guarantee' to hold a referendum on any treaty emerging from the Lisbon process if he became prime minister, and staked his premiership on the outcome (Ashcroft and Oakeshott, 2016: 564). He specifically identified immigration as an issue on which he detected growing public concern. At the Conservative Party conference in 2007, he acknowledged: 'I think our diverse and multi-racial society is a huge benefit for Britain, but we do have to recognise the pressures that can be put on public services, schools and hospitals and housing if immigration is unlimited.'

While still in opposition, in 2009, Cameron dropped his pledge to hold a referendum on the Lisbon Treaty when it was ratified by all the other EU member states and by the Labour government. However, he maintained that, if elected in 2010, no future substantial transfer of powers would take place without the consent of the British people (Westlake, 2017: 12). In 2009, the UK Independence party (UKIP), which had put an in/out referendum on UK membership of the EU at the heart of its programme, came second in the European Parliament elections with 18 seats and 16.5% of UK votes on a turnout of 34.3%. UKIP was ahead of Labour in votes but on a par with them for seats. This result convinced the Conservatives, with 27.4% of the votes and 36 seats, that they badly needed to counteract the threat posed by UKIP's policy on issues such as immigration.

The inevitability of a UK referendum on Europe

When Cameron came to power in May 2010, with a more eurosceptic generation of members of parliament, he was hoping to prevent his premiership from being defined by the Europe question (Seldon and Snowdon, 2016: 165). His intention in coalition with the Liberal Democrats was to roll back unnecessary EU legislation and build long-term alliances with like-minded member states, while seeking to retain the UK's influence in shaping EU policy.

Chapter 12 of the Coalition European Union Act 2011 laid down restrictions on treaties and decisions relating to the EU. The purpose of the bill was to amend the European Communities Act 1972 so that any proposed future treaty that transferred areas of power, or competences, would be subject to a referendum. Article 48(6) of the Treaty on the Functioning of the European Union

(TFEU) specified cases where a decision of the Council required approval by a referendum or parliamentary act, including social security, social protection and social policy. The 2011 Act established a 'referendum lock' to prevent another Lisbon.

Early in his mandate, Cameron's seemingly good intentions to ensure that the UK played a lead role in developing EU integration from the inside were thwarted by the eurozone crisis, where the UK was an outsider. Nor did he seem to understand the extent to which his decision in 2011 to take the Conservative Party out of the European People's Party (EPP) in the European Parliament would be interpreted as a betrayal by the German Chancellor, Angela Merkel, thereby 'beginning the process of disentanglement from Brussels' (Ashcroft and Oakeshott, 2016: 498–9).

Cameron's cooperative approach on Europe was further jeopardised in the discussions about the next presidency of the Commission in 2014. He strongly opposed the candidacy (as *Spitzenkandidat*) of Jean-Claude Juncker, a former prime minister of Luxembourg, an *ex officio* vice-president of the EPP, and a federalist. Juncker was known to favour a social model of Europe that was out of tune with the direction that Cameron wanted to take. In his view, Juncker's appointment would increase support for a British withdrawal from the EU (Watt and Traynor, 2014).

Although, in his 2013 Bloomberg speech before a domestic audience, Cameron advocated continuing membership of the EU, he was fully aware of growing public euroscepticism, the need for democratic accountability, bureaucratic reform, the removal of spurious legislation, and greater recognition of national specificities. He portrayed the UK as 'a country which in many ways invented the single market, and which brings real heft to Europe's influence on the world stage which plays by the rules and which is a force for liberal economic reform', without which, he maintained, it 'would be a very different kind of European Union'. Echoing the words of his predecessors, and foreshadowing those of his successor, he stressed the importance of protecting national interests. He argued against 'ever closer union' but in favour of reform of the eurozone and single market, more subsidiarity and more constraints on EU institutions. He wanted to prevent the vast flow of migrants and ensure a greater role for national parliaments. Social and employment policy, as well as the single market and free movement of persons were included as key areas for a review of the balance of competences between the UK and the EU commissioned by the coalition (HM Government, 2014a, 2014b).

On this basis, Cameron committed to holding a referendum on EU membership if the Conservatives won the next election but only after he had renegotiated the UK's relationship with the EU. Arguably, this decision helped, at least temporarily, to restore unity within the Conservative Party and to 'spike' the growing popularity of UKIP (Seldon and Snowdon, 2016: 544–5). With 26.6% of the votes cast on a turnout of 35.6%, UKIP had gained the largest number of UK seats (24) in the 2014 European Parliament elections.

Meanwhile, two referendums in other member states confirmed that euroscepticism was not confined to the British public. A referendum in July 2015 on the bailout conditions in the Greek sovereign-debt crisis was rejected by 61.3% of voters, although, shortly afterwards, the government accepted a bailout with even harsher conditions. A referendum was held in Denmark in December 2015 to decide on converting their opt-out from participation in the area of Justice and Home Affairs into an opt-in, by allowing Danish voters the possibility to decide on a case-by-case basis. The proposal was rejected with 51.3% against.

The social dimension and the 2016 referendum

When the Conservatives won a majority in the House of Commons in the 2015 general election, enabling them to govern without the Liberal Democrats, Cameron immediately pledged to carry out his election manifesto promise to hold a referendum on the UK's membership of the EU by the end of 2017. This section examines the role played by the social dimension in Cameron's attempt to secure changes to EU rules and in the referendum campaign, particularly regarding migration.

Renegotiating the relationship with the EU

In his Chatham House speech in 2015, Cameron outlined four main objectives, all of which could have an impact on social policy development, and which he hoped would appeal to the electorate. He undertook to protect the single market for the UK and others outside the eurozone; write competitiveness into the DNA of the whole EU, including cutting the total burden on business; exempt the UK from an 'ever closer union' and bolster national parliaments through legally binding and irreversible changes; tackle abuses of the right to free movement, and enable the UK to control migration from the EU. Before holding a referendum, Cameron had to fulfil his commitment to renegotiate the UK's relationship with the EU.

In preparing for the February 2016 summit in Brussels, Cameron presented what he saw as achievable aims in response to the concerns being enflamed by UKIP: a ban on EU migrants claiming child benefit for offspring not living in the UK; a ban on migrants collecting work-related benefits and a binding opt-out from the commitment to 'ever closer union' (Ashcroft and Oakeshott, 2016: 545). He was overly optimistic that the other heads of state or government would endorse the stance he was taking thereby enabling him to convince the UK electorate of the case for remaining in the EU.

As part of a package of changes sought to EU rules, his proposal to operate an 'emergency brake' (officially an 'alert and safeguard mechanism') for social protection benefits received a favourable hearing. Against the background of the EU's immigration crisis, other member states were prepared to restrict rights to social protection for mobile workers and their families in specific circumstances, as reported in the European Council Conclusions

(EUCO 1/16). The heads of state or government agreed to amend Regulation (EC) No 883/2004 on the coordination of social security systems by introducing an option to index 'exported' child benefits 'to the conditions of the member state where the child resides' (EUCO 1/16: annex V). They thus overruled EEC Treaty article 51, which prescribed that workers and their families should qualify for benefits according to 'the respective municipal law of the [host] countries concerned'. In addition, Cameron secured an exemption for the UK from the notion of 'ever closer union' being written into the treaties at a future date.

Views on what Cameron achieved at the February summit differed markedly between EU allies and the UK press and Brexiteers (Ashcroft and Oakeshott, 2016: 546–8; Evans and Menon, 2017: 47–8). Other member states considered that the deal represented a significant concession on the part of the EU, and, for Emmanuel Macron, the French president, even that it went too far (Rogers, 2018: 259). Cameron and many of his advisers did not, however, appreciate until it was too late that the terms agreed would not be enough to meet the UK electorate's expectations or to placate the eurosceptic press (Barnard, 2017: 496; Seldon and Snowdon, 2016: 553).

Nor had the efforts by the European Commission to extend the reach of social policy beyond employment rights convinced the electorate in the UK that the protection given to citizens by the EU, or its contribution to their quality of life, were sufficient to counter negative opinions about the impact of migration and to make them aware of the advantages of remaining within the EU (Eurobarometer, 2015). After Cameron's failure to secure an 'acceptable' deal for a domestic audience at the Brussels summit, in a speech to the House of Commons on 22 February 2016, he announced that the referendum would be held on 23 June 2016. The electorate would be asked: 'Should the United Kingdom remain a member of the European Union or leave the European Union?' He expressed his conviction that the UK would be 'safer, stronger and better off by remaining in a reformed European Union'.

The social dimension in the referendum campaign

Although social policies have usually been subordinated to economic issues, they have often served as an indicator of underlying causes of dissension. Cameron's team decided early on to fight the Remain campaign on the economic risks of the UK leaving the EU. As the indicators pointed more compellingly towards the negative impact on the economy of a vote to leave, the Leave campaign switched its focus to immigration, which the Remain campaign was avoiding, since the Conservatives felt unable to find an answer on the issue (Ashcroft and Oakeshott, 2016: 551; Seldon and Snowdon, 2016: 550–1).

Jeremy Corbyn, the leader of the opposition from 2015, had been a lifelong left-wing eurosceptic. He had voted to leave in the 1975 referendum, and voted against the SEA, Maastricht and Lisbon Treaties when they were ratified in parliament. He publicly supported the Remain campaign, although his view of the EU was of a 'rich man's capitalist club that allowed lobbyists and business interests to collude against workers'; any show of Labour unity was a 'façade' (Ashcroft and Oakeshott, 2016: 551, 553).

In support of the case for EU intervention, on the eve of the referendum, the TUC issued a paper in which it enumerated the significant employment rights gains that had, in its opinion, accrued to UK workers as a result of EU membership, due largely to the alliances built across the EU. The TUC (2016: 3) warned that British workers would be particularly vulnerable if the UK left the EU.

During the campaign, divisions within the political parties, reinforced by the claims and counterclaims of Leavers and Remainers, made it difficult to predict how the public would vote and what the implications of Brexit might be for UK and EU policy, not least in the social domain. Analysts of the innumerable surveys and opinion polls recognised the importance of prior convictions rather than impartial assessments by voters of the arguments put forward in the campaign (Evans and Menon, 2017:

87–8). For the public in the UK the EC/EU had never been 'a decisive political issue'; relative disinterest had coexisted with limited support. Interest grew, however, as immigration became increasingly associated with negative attitudes towards the EU and its social provisions, fanned by UKIP (Evans and Menon, 2017: 16–22, 42).

After six years of austerity leading to cuts in public services and the failure to resolve chronic housing shortages, migration had become a 'convenient scapegoat', providing 'the focus for public dissatisfaction, a vector for their anger often about other matters such as precarity' (Barnard, 2017: 478, 483). Some critics expected immigration to be more difficult to control from within the EU, which had also been urging austerity and had contributed to hardship in the eurozone countries, as patently demonstrated by the Greek case. The threat of more harmonisation and a relentless shift towards the EU as a superstate also became persuasive arguments for leaving (Evans and Menon, 2017: 80).

The social dimension in the referendum outcome and withdrawal negotiations

Even in the 1950s, the question of EEC membership 'did not sit comfortably into the standard left versus right, state versus market structure of political debate'; nor could the 'sovereignty versus interdependence' cleavage in the 1960s be organised along traditional party lines (Rosamond, 2007: 59). This section examines the role played by underlying social issues in determining the results of the referendum and the place of enduring social concerns in the withdrawal negotiations.

The social dimension in the referendum outcome

With a 72.2% turnout, 51.89% of those who voted in the 2016 referendum chose to leave and 48.11% to remain. Analysis of voting patterns in the referendum by political scientists confirms that voting did not divide along traditional left–right lines (Evans and Menon, 2017: 64; Curtice and Tipping, 2018: 4), suggesting that it would be 'an extremely difficult task to unite the country behind a future EU relationship when the moment comes for decisions to replace rhetoric' (Harding, 2018).

A clear message was the importance of the role that the erosion of faith in politics played in the outcome (Evans and Menon, 2017: 70). After several years of austerity, the referendum gave the public an opportunity to express its general frustration and discontent with UK and EU governance of whatever political persuasion. Poverty and inequality were important for Leave voters, particularly for those with few or no qualifications. Immigration and the economy were shown to be interconnected. Remainers, for their part, were overwhelmingly concerned about the economic consequences of Brexit along with its impact on employment and social rights (Evans and Menon, 2017: 75–7).

A marked level of stability was found in opinions before and after the campaign coalescing around values about order, authority, morality and freedom, which were not closely reflected in traditional political views (Evans and Menon, 2017: 73). The long-running (since 1983) British Social Attitudes (BSA) survey provided insights into how public attitudes towards the EU evolved prior to and following the referendum (Curtice and Tipping 2018: 6–7). From the late 1990s, eurosceptic respondents were more likely to agree that the UK should remain in the EU but should seek to reduce its powers. From 1998, the public became increasingly eurosceptic, reaching two thirds or more of respondents from 2012 and peaking at 78% in 2016. At that time, a larger proportion of eurosceptics supported leaving: 41% compared to 22% in 2015 and 36% in 2017. Whereas 43% supported the reform option in 2015 when Cameron was planning to renegotiate the relationship with the EU, the proportion had fallen back to 33% in 2017 when article 50 was triggered.

The 2017 BSA survey produced little evidence that the EU referendum campaign had made UK respondents less tolerant towards migrants. Rather, they had come to be valued for their contribution to the economy and to cultural life (Curtice and Tipping, 2018: 13–14). However, the Brexit process did reveal a significant and growing divide within society by age and education. More of the better educated and younger (aged under 35) voters, particularly among women, supported Remain, while more of the older (aged over 55) less educated voters, particularly among women, supported Leave (Skinner and Gottfried, 2016; Curtice and Tipping, 2018: 22). Paradoxically, regions that voted most strongly for Leave, notably in Wales and the North East, tended to be those most dependent on EU markets and on EU financial support for their local economic development (Evans and Menon, 2017: 111; Outhwaite, 2017: vii). Analysis of the BSA 2017 findings led to the conclusion that:

> What [voters] do seem to have done during the referendum campaign – and since – is to align their views more closely, not just to their perceptions of some of the consequences of leaving the EU, but also to their sense of identity and whether they uphold a socially liberal outlook or a more conservative one. [This may explain] why voters in Britain have so far emerged from the Brexit process more critical of Britain's membership of the EU. Those whose perceptions, sense of identity and values already predisposed them in 2015 to take a sceptical view of the EU have particularly come to the view that the UK should leave. (Curtice and Tipping, 2018: 24)

The social dimension in the withdrawal negotiations

In the early stages of the negotiations, the public and EU negotiators wanted the UK government to explain what it meant by Brexit. Prime Minister Theresa May consistently asserted that 'Brexit means Brexit' (Richards, 2018), but without being overly specific in clarifying whether all links with the EU would be broken or what Brexit would mean for everyday life.

In her 2017 Lancaster House speech, May laid down the principles that would govern the negotiations. In the social area, she stressed the intention to control immigration to the UK from the EU, while guaranteeing the rights of EU citizens already living in the UK. Workers' rights would be fully protected and maintained. A few months later, the government's 2017 White Paper on *The United Kingdom's exit from and new partnership with the European Union* confirmed the government's intention to seek a 'clean break', meaning taking back control of its own statute book and bringing an end to the jurisdiction of the CJEU. The Great Repeal Bill would

> remove the European Communities Act 1972 from the statute book and convert the 'acquis' – the body of existing EU law – into domestic law. ... mean[ing,] that, wherever practical and appropriate, the same rules and laws will apply on the day after we leave the EU as they did before. (2017 White Paper, section 1.1)

More explicitly:

> The Government's general approach to preserving EU law is to ensure that all EU laws which are directly applicable in the UK (such as EU regulations) and all laws which have been made in the UK, in order to implement our obligations as a member of the EU, remain part of domestic law on the day we leave the EU. (2017 White Paper: 10)

The government responded to pressures from the trades unions by indicating that it would retain some of the most contentious EU social legislation. Among the examples selected to illustrate the government's intentions to repeal or amend legislation, the 2017 White Paper identified the protection of workers' rights as one (number 7) of its 12 guiding principles to be applied 'in fulfilling the democratic will of the people of the UK'. The stated aim was to protect and enhance 'existing workers' rights'. The White Paper cited the parental leave arrangements and holiday entitlement (§7.2) in the UK as specific instances where UK employment law exceeded EU legislation by applying higher standards. Only in the case of intra-EU migration did the government unambiguously assert that the so-called Free Movement Directive (2004/38/EC) would no longer apply from day one, and that the migration of EU nationals would henceforth be subject to UK law (§5.4). In her letter to Donald Tusk, the President of the European Council, triggering article 50, May assured UK and EU citizens in other member states that the UK government would 'aim to strike an early agreement about their rights'; it would foster 'a deep and special partnership between the UK and the EU' based on 'close regulatory alignment'.

A year later, the negotiations had stalled, and divisions within the political parties were as stark as ever. In her 2018 Mansion House speech, May remained adamant, asserting that 'free movement of people will come to an end'. She reiterated the message that, in the social domain, the UK expected to retain and enhance existing regulatory standards whatever the nature of the future trading relationship and organisational links between the UK and its EU neighbours.

Social policy and the repeal of EU law

To ensure a smooth transition after 29 March 2019 when the UK was due to exit the EU, arrangements were made in the European Union (Withdrawal) Act 2018 to repeal the European Communities Act 1972 and the European Union Act 2011. The 2018 Act provided for the retention of most of repealed law, by 'converting' or 'transposing' it into a freestanding body of domestic law, adopting a rulebook for institutional arrangements initially as close as possible to existing law (Cowie, 2018: 4–5).

In the Withdrawal Act 2018, retained law covered EU regulations (some 20,000 in total), most notably in the social domain those concerning the coordination of social security rights of migrant workers and their families, where agreement was reached by December 2017 guaranteeing the rights enshrined in Regulation (EC) No 883/2004. Retained law disapplied the principle of supremacy of EU law for prospective legislation, and excluded EU directives, as opposed to implementation legislation, since directives are not directly applicable in UK law. Although the Charter of Fundamental Rights of the EU did not form part of retained EU law, some of the rights included could be kept, insofar as they appear elsewhere in retained EU law (Cowie, 2018: 32–4).

Much of the social legislation that became part of the *acquis communautaire* from the 1990s following the Maastricht Treaty was adopted as secondary legislation under heads other than those requiring unanimous voting (directives rather than regulations): health and safety, working conditions, gender equality and human rights. For the purposes of the Withdrawal Act, EU-derived domestic law meant legislation enacted by the UK parliament or government to give effect to, or support, the implementation of EU law in the UK, such as the UK's 1998 working time legislation, implementing EU directive 93/104/EC. It also provided for the effective implementation of rights arising directly under the treaties, for instance the UK Equality Act 2010, which had the same objectives as the EU's main equal treatment directives (Cowie, 2018: 19–20).

Detailing the Chequers' agreement a few days earlier, the 12 July 2018 White Paper on *The future relationship between the United Kingdom and the European Union* reaffirmed that the government was 'committing to high levels of social and employment protections through a non-regression requirement for domestic labour standards' (§108e). The White Paper (§121) reiterated that for intra-EU migrants: 'Existing workers' rights enjoyed under EU law will continue to be available in UK law on the day of withdrawal.' This commitment was repeated in the *Agreement on the withdrawal of the United Kingdom from the European Union*, as endorsed by leaders at a special meeting of the European Council on 25 November 2018.

Part Two of the Agreement on Citizens' Rights set out detailed provisions for equal treatment and opportunities between men and women, migrant workers and their family members in employment, occupation, qualifications and social security during and at the end of the transition period. The Political Declaration, accompanying the Agreement, offered a framework for the UK's future relationship with the EU in the form of a 'flexible partnership', based on: mutual interest and cooperation, for example through participation in EU education, science and innovation programmes; shared values, the rule of law and high standards of workers' and citizenship rights, public health and social services; and a balance of rights and obligations, designed to safeguard sovereignty, the promotion and protection of cultural diversity, and the ending of free movement (§§ 1–7, 11–12, 14, 17–18). Arrangements were to be considered to provide for mobility (Part II section IX) and to tackle illegal migration (Part III section IV D).

The implications of Brexit for UK social policy

In anticipation of the referendum result, and foreshadowing objections to the eventual adoption, post-Brexit, of the 'Norwegian model', Cameron acknowledged in his 2013 Bloomberg speech that, even if the UK left the EU completely and lost all remaining vetoes and a voice in negotiations, decisions made at European level would continue to have a profound effect on the country. Stephen Wall, a former UK Permanent Representative to the EU had argued a decade earlier:

> There would be a huge loss to British interests if twenty-six other countries were taking, without us, decisions … when those decisions would in all cases bear directly on our national interest and … have to be implemented in Britain simply because we would otherwise be unable to operate in the European market place. (Wall, 2008: 210)

Arguably, by transposing most of EU law into domestic law, the immediate impact of withdrawal on UK social legislation would be minimal for a number of reasons: the UK parliament's Scrutiny Committee always carefully scrutinised EU law before agreeing to it (Wall, 2008: 218); the UK government insisted on implementing directives in ways that did not conflict with the national interest;

it committed to maintaining high social standards whatever the outcome of the negotiations; the government would face strong opposition from trades unions and left-wing voters if social rights risked being flaunted; employers in the public and private sectors objected strongly to any reversal of social legislation that they had implemented at great expense (British Chambers of Commerce, 2017: 12); and unravelling many decades of social legislation and deciding what to keep and what to reject would be unmanageable.

Opinion was divided about the impact of Brexit on UK social policy in the medium and longer term. For the German political scientist and close observer of the UK, Antje Wiener (2017: 141, 149), the EU having become more than an international organisation of states, disentanglement of legislation, regulations and procedures would be extremely complex if not impossible in the unprecedented situation created by Brexit. She described it as a 'nightmare' for politicians and a cause of heightened alienation for voters. Wiener also identified an 'underestimation' by UK politicians and voters of 'what the EU has become after more than five decades of integration', and how participation in that process had changed the UK 'and with it the British people'.

Policy analysts considering the longer term argued that the UK would feel the effects of Brexit in areas of employment equality, anti-discrimination legislation, freedom of movement, regional development, health and social care (Kennett, 2017: 440–1; Stewart, Cooper and Shutes, 2019). More specifically, deregulation of the labour market would affect gender equality (Fagan and Rubery, 2018: 312), employment rights (TUC, 2016), and the rights of migrant workers and their families (D'Angelo and Kofmann, 2018).

The evidence accumulated in this chapter and in Chapter 3 suggests that the long-term impact of Brexit on social policy would be likely to depend not only on the nature of the future relationship – the close friendship and strong partnership – being sought between the UK and EU27 but also on the ability of future UK governments to deliver social policies that could heal the many fractures in society exposed by the referendum.

FIVE

Brexit and EU social policy

Both before and since the establishment of the European Economic Community (EEC) in 1957, decisions were taken about the principles and development of the EEC's social dimension without the participation of the UK. When the six founding member states were drafting the EEC Treaty, the UK was exploring various options and was absent from much of the debate about Europe. The French then vetoed the UK's application to join the EEC for a further 15 years. As an outsider, the UK was not party to any of the decisions taken during that time, but it was compelled to give existing EEC social law supremacy over national law as a condition of membership on joining the EEC in 1973. As with every new wave of membership, European institutions sought to negotiate compromises and trade-offs in the social domain to avoid 'a race to the bottom' and to achieve their long-term aim of coordinating a greater diversity of social systems.

From inside the EC, successive UK prime ministers rejected or opted out of European social legislation and programmes that they considered counter to the national interest. Most notably, the UK did not sign up to the 1989 Community Charter of the Fundamental Social Rights of Workers and the Agreement on

Social Policy (referred to as the Social Chapter) when the Community Charter was incorporated into the Maastricht Treaty in 1992 as the European Union's (EU) social dimension. With Denmark, Ireland and Italy, in 1985 the UK declined to sign up to the Schengen Agreement on passport-free borders within the EEC. Although the UK government belatedly joined the Exchange Rate Mechanism (ERM) in 1989, with Italy it was forced to withdraw in 1992 when the pound and lira crashed. With Denmark and Sweden, the UK did not join the euro when it was launched in 1999. During his premiership, under pressure from eurosceptics, John Major negotiated the UK government into a position in the social domain where the other member states could go ahead without the UK. His actions meant that the UK had effectively excluded itself from participating in decisions about key interconnected areas of European economic and social policy.

Read in conjunction with the two previous chapters, this chapter shows how, when the UK was absent from the negotiating table, European institutions brought forward proposals that had been blocked, or at least, delayed, due largely to the UK's opposition, prefiguring reactions to the UK's permanent departure from the EU. Drawing on examples of actions taken at EU level without the UK, the chapter considers:

- how the Commission reacted in 1992 when the UK rejected the Agreement on Social Policy in the Maastricht Treaty and withdrew from the ERM;
- how EU institutions responded to euroscepticism heightened by the global financial and eurozone crises;
- how, with the UK and Ireland outside the Schengen Agreement, EU member states reacted to the immigration crisis;
- how the European Commission anticipated Brexit by taking forward initiatives in the social domain;
- in light of these findings, what the UK's withdrawal might mean for the future development of European social policy.

Chapter 4 considered the impact of Brexit on the relationship between the UK and the EU in the social policy domain from the UK's perspective. This chapter focusses on the possible implications of Brexit for EU institutions and the remaining 27 member states. The withdrawal negotiations were conducted between what was initially portrayed as a united EU and a single unified member state. In reality, the 2016 UK referendum exacerbated existing deep divisions in the UK over Europe making it extremely difficult to reach a common position. But nor did the EU constitute a homogenous social union, meaning that any process of mutual disentanglement would be long and arduous.

Managing European social policy without the UK

As an EU member state, the UK developed a sound record for compliance with EU legislation: for example, it was consistently less often implicated in infringement procedures than France, Germany or Italy (European Commission, 2016). The UK was not alone in resorting to opt-outs and delaying tactics to prevent the dilution of national sovereignty in the social field. It built alliances with like-minded countries and provided a lead for other member states opposed to further encroachment of EU competence in the social domain. This section examines how EU institutions sought to take forward social policy when the UK was absent from the negotiating table in the 1990s.

Learning to live without the UK in the social domain

Various interpretations have been proposed to explain the impact of Prime Minister Margaret Thatcher's aggressive 'negotiating style'. One explanation holds that her apparent unwillingness to compromise enabled her to exact larger concessions than might otherwise not have been possible. The UK came to be recognised as one of the most effective players in getting what it wanted (Oliver, 2018: 44). At European summits, Thatcher's adversarial stance meant that like-minded member states could rely on the UK to oppose any proposals allowing expansion of Community competence in the social domain. When, in 1983, Thatcher was momentarily more concerned about completing the Single European Market (SEM) than protecting national sovereignty, Denmark was left alone to express its reservations about plans to deepen and broaden the scope of European activities (European Council, 1983: §§3.1.1, 3.4.3, 4.2).

When Major opted out of the Social Chapter in the Maastricht Treaty in an attempt both to broker a compromise within the divided Conservative Party, and to avert the threat of new regulatory burdens on industry, the UK was effectively excluded from social policy negotiations for five years. The Liberal Democrats in the UK accused Major of condemning the country to being 'semi-detached' from Europe, and Labour claimed that the UK had isolated itself from the rest of Europe (Wall, 2008: 137).

At a joint press conference with Major in 1992, Jacques Delors, the President of the European Commission, responded to a question from a BBC journalist by affirming that: 'The twelve member states accepted the two opting out in the Maastricht summit [Denmark had opted out of Economic and Monetary Union, EMU]. This is not the first time there was an opting-out and it is frankly possible to manage the Community and to make progress in those conditions.'

By putting the UK in the position of rule-taker rather than rule-maker, the five years from 1992 to 1997 tested the theory that the UK government was the main obstacle to the advancement of EU social policy. For some observers (Hooghe and Marks, 2008: 21; Westlake, 2017: 14; Oliver, 2018: 7; Stuart, 2018), 1992 initiated euroscepticism and marked an irrevocable step along the path to Brexit. For the Commission and other member states, it provided an opportunity to discover what the UK's permanent absence from the negotiating table might mean for EU social policy development and, in the longer term, for European social integration.

Taking advantage of UK social policy opt-outs

As claimed by Delors, the Commission was already accustomed to looking for ways of avoiding confrontation with heads of state or government. The Community's 1994 White Paper on *European social policy: A way forward for the European Union* (COM(94)333) set out a far-reaching social policy agenda. It proposed legislation and action programmes in areas of health and safety at work that no longer required unanimous voting. It also introduced alternative procedures and instruments to hard law, such as the open method of coordination (OMC), a form of soft governance designed to unlock social and employment policies.

While the UK was away from the negotiating table, the social partners – Union of Industrial and Employers' Confederations of Europe (UNICE, now Business Europe), European Centre of Employers and Enterprises (CEEP) and European Trade Union Confederation (ETUC) – took advantage of the UK's absence to bring forward health and safety directives under 'framework agreements', introduced as part of the European social dialogue autonomous process. Three such agreements were implemented as Council directives: on parental leave (96/34/EC), part-time work (97/81/EC) and fixed-term contracts (99/70/EC). As Paymaster General in 1985, Kenneth Clarke had blocked a proposal for statutory paternity leave (George, 1998: 187), which the Parental Leave Directive unblocked.

Other contentious social legislation that progressed during the UK's absence included the Pregnant Workers' Directive (92/85/EEC), which had originally been conceived as an equality measure under EEC Treaty article 119; and the Working Time Directive (93/104/EC), which was repealed and codified a decade later (2003/88/EC). Ivor Richard (1983), the UK's Commissioner for Employment, Social Affairs, Education and Training, had earlier sought to promote these policies during his term in office (1981–85), but they had remained on the table for over a decade due largely to UK opposition (Burrows and Mair, 1996: 279).

When Tony Blair, as prime minister, agreed to be bound by the provisions of the Social Chapter, it was incorporated into the 1997 Consolidated EU Treaty. The Treaty legally endorsed the commitment of all member states to develop the social dimension as an important component in the process of European integration. Since directives are implemented at national level, the UK's temporary absence from the negotiating table did not prevent it from choosing how to transpose legislation into national law, providing such law achieved the required result.

The amended version of the Working Time Directive (2003/88/EC) left open the possibility for individual workers to opt out of the 48-hour restriction. By 2010, 16 member states made provision for an opt-out, including France and Germany (European Commission, 2010: 88). When the European Parliament sought revisions to the directive in 2009, opposition was led by the UK government. Employers blocked a second attempt in 2010 under the social dialogue procedure. Efforts by the Commission to extend the provisions of the Pregnant Workers' Directive in 2008 failed to secure the Council's support (Bailey, 2017: 118). In 2017, the European Parliament launched a controversial proposal for a work–life balance directive (Milotay, 2018).

These examples indicate that the UK's influence could still be felt even when it was not directly involved in negotiations. They also demonstrate that the UK government was not alone in blocking, contesting or delaying social measures.

EU social policy and euroscepticism

Much has been written, particularly since the 1990s about the 'democratic deficit', meaning the lack of legitimacy and accountability of EU institutions, as manifested in the unprecedented rise both of euroscepticism and of anti-European political parties (Kassim, 2007: 188–93; Baker and Schnapper, 2015: 114–16). This section considers how euroscepticism developed in EU member states, and was exacerbated by the actions of EU institutions during the global financial crisis and the ensuing eurozone sovereign-debt crisis between 2008 and 2011, with the UK outside the eurozone.

Explaining the spread of euroscepticism

In the context of economic recession of the early 1970s euroscepticism was present in the member states even as the UK joined. The Community's 'democratic' credentials were called into question during the 1980s with the adoption of the Single European Act (SEA). Scepticism about the ability of the EU to deliver policies that serve the interests of its peoples had become widespread by the time the UK opted out of the Social Chapter in 1992. Euroscepticism grew rapidly when further treaty reforms were proposed, as demonstrated when electorates were given an opportunity to ratify treaty changes in referendums. For example, the French and Dutch electorates rejected the Constitutional Treaty in 2005, by 54.7% and 61.5% respectively, due mainly in the French case to the fear of losing their social model, and in the Dutch case to the threat posed to their national cultural identity (Binzer Hobolt and Brouard, 2011: 319).

As the impact of the global financial crisis on EU member states became clearer, the Commission sought to counter euroscepticism by using 'stronger EU-level coordination to avoid competitive distortions in the internal market' and to ease 'the social hardship stemming from recession' (European Commission, 2009: 75, 82). The sovereign-debt crisis then compounded the effects of the financial crisis moving several countries from surplus to deficit.

By intervening at intergovernmental level in the worst affected eurozone countries, the Troika (Commission, European Central Bank and International Monetary Fund) not only side-lined EU law, they also undermined national autonomy. The Troika insisted that sovereign-debt crisis countries should undertake structural reforms to their domestic labour and social security laws to restore fiscal balances. The depression of wages and the reduction in the cost of social security systems in debtor countries became a condition for accessing bailouts (Deakin, 2017: 199), even though, in principle, national governments retained the right to decide how to cut public spending and increase public revenue (Lenaerts and Gutiérrez-Fons, 2017: 437, 454). Austerity measures and widespread welfare retrenchment called into question the authority of EU institutions. The level of contestation peaked across EU member states in the wake of the financial crises, resulting in open expressions of euroscepticism and disaffection with the European project, particularly in Denmark, France and the UK (Pollack, Wallace and Young, 2015: 474–5), although these were not the countries worst affected by the financial crisis.

In the 2014 European Parliament elections, an estimated 30 eurosceptic political parties from 18 member states gained a total of 125 seats, constituting 16.6% of total members (Bertoncini and Koenig, 2014: 1). Eurobarometer surveys for 2015 show that, across the EU as a whole, the proportion of respondents with a positive image of the EU fell from a high of 52% in early 2007 to 38% in 2010 before rising to 41% in 2015 (Eurobarometer, 2015: 112). Trust in the EU, having peaked at 57% in early 2007, fell to 31% in 2012 and stood at 40% in 2015 (Eurobarometer, 2015: 106). However, in no country did more than 50% of respondents believe that they would be better able to face the future outside the EU in 2015. In the UK, the same proportion (43%) of respondents agreed and disagreed with the proposition (Eurobarometer, 2015: 99).

EU responses to global financial and eurozone crises

EU institutions have long been concerned about their public image and legitimacy, as well as their ability to deliver accountability. As demonstrated in Chapter 3, the UK played an important role in helping the Commission to refine the monitoring tools that the Commission now uses routinely to assess not only the performance of member states but also its own record. In combination, the global financial and eurozone sovereign-debt crises severely shook the confidence of European citizens in the ability of politicians and bureaucrats to govern.

In the wake of these crises, EU institutions realised that they needed to pay more attention to their 'social conscience'. Against a background of global economic disruption caused by the oil crises in the early 1970s, as Director-General for Social Affairs (1973–76), Michael Shanks, a UK national, was responsible for formulating and delivering the Commission's first social action programme in 1974. Using words that resonate across the decades, in presenting the programme, Shanks (1973: 2) emphasised the need for Europe to concentrate 'on improving the quality of life, on improving the human face of the Community, and on an approach which is far more attentive to the social aspects of Community policies than that laid down by the Treaty of Rome'.

In 2013, in response to growing hostility across the EU, and in the knowledge that the UK would not be alone in opposing further encroachment in national social space, the Commission avoided the hard law route and focussed on reviving economic growth, reducing unemployment and improving employability by 'investing in people'. The aim of the Social Investment Package (SIP), launched in 2013, was to 'absolve the trade-off between states and markets, between equality and efficiency, and between social and economic goals' (Kvist, 2017: 75, 87). The Commission identified key policy areas for attention, comprising not only job-search assistance, rehabilitation, education and training, but also quality child care and health care. It adopted a life-course perspective to add value and spread benefits to less privileged categories of the population by investing in the future.

The Commission's 2013 Communication on social investment for growth and cohesion (COM(2013)83 final) offered member states guidance on how best to use EU financial support, notably from the European Social Fund (ESF), to achieve more efficient and effective social budgeting. The Commission undertook to monitor closely the performance of individual member states' social protection systems through the European Semester, which had been introduced in 2010. The Semester provided a framework for discussing national economic and budget plans at specific times throughout the year and for coordinating economic policies. The SIP aimed to achieve better coordination of national social security schemes by using monitoring tools such as social indicators and benchmarks. Where necessary, the Commission formulates country-specific recommendations. Through the SIP and European Semester, the original emphasis in European social policy shifted from considering the social dimension as an output of market integration: it became an input into sustainable economic development (Deakin, 2017: 210).

Some governments found monitoring intrusive and saw it as an attempt to push the limits of EU competence too far. For others, monitoring was accepted as a logical outcome of efforts to develop alternatives to hard law. As a form of soft law akin to the OMC, member states are not required to submit their plans to the SIP for regulatory scrutiny, and they are not obliged to accept the EU's recommendations. The UK's absence or presence from the SIP does not therefore have much impact on other member states except insofar as the UK provided examples of good practices. In 2009, for instance, the European Commission (2009: 76) cited the UK for its adoption of a comprehensive strategy on employment as a social protection crisis measure.

EU perspectives on migration policy and Brexit

As one of the three EU member states (with Ireland and Sweden) that opened its borders to migrants from the Central and Eastern European (CEE) accession countries in 2004, the UK received disproportionately large numbers of CEE migrants. Migration was to play a major role in the referendum campaign and, at least initially, in the withdrawal negotiations, although, unlike most other EU member states, neither the UK public nor its government explicitly distinguished between third-country and intra-European migration. While the EU was striving to restore its public image in the wake of the financial and eurozone crises, member states faced a different challenge from migration as more than a million migrants and refugees crossed into Europe in 2015. This section considers how the UK was positioned in the debates over intra-European and third-country migration; how, without the UK and Ireland, the Schengen countries sought to resolve the refugee crisis; and why intra-European freedom of movement became one of the red lines in the Brexit negotiations.

Regulating migration in the EU

In the EEC Treaty, under the title providing for the Free Movement of Persons, Services and Capital, four articles were devoted to ensuring both that mobile 'workers' would not be discriminated against, and that their right to benefits accumulated during their working lives would be protected. Some of the earliest regulations (the most binding form of European legislation) gave the EU the power to 'coordinate' the social security systems of member states through cooperation and mutual recognition of one another's systems, thereby constraining the scope for member states to determine qualifying conditions for social security benefits. Intra-EU migration thus became an area where the EU could act to remove barriers to free movement. By overriding the unanimity rule for social security, it could regulate national legislation governing access to social protection benefits and services for migrants and their families.

The EEC Treaty did not make provision for third-country migration. In the 1980s, the main concern of EU member states had been to present a common position on third-country asylum seekers. The founding member states, except for Italy, signed the Schengen Agreement on asylum and visas in 1985. The Agreement was due to be implemented by 1994, following ratification by the 13 participating countries, including by that stage Italy, Greece,

Portugal, Spain, Austria, Finland and Sweden. Ireland and the UK did not sign up to Schengen, and Denmark negotiated a partial opt-out. Under the Agreement, signatory countries agreed to abolish internal EU border controls, to adopt common visa procedures for asylum-seekers and to expand police cooperation.

Ireland and the UK also declined to sign up to the 1990 Dublin Convention (or Regulation), which took effect in 1997, and was subsequently amended in 2003. Denmark obtained an opt-out from the implementing regulations. Dublin determined the EU member state responsible for examining applications for asylum. The Dublin Convention was designed to prevent 'asylum shopping' by requiring asylum seekers to register in the first country that they reached (Hansen, 2007: 342).

The UK agreed to the integration of the Schengen system into the framework of the EU legal order under the Treaty of Amsterdam in 1999, thereby enabling it to enter into force as a Justice and Home Affairs measure, and to be brought under the jurisdiction of the CJEU. Articles 79 and 80 of the 2007 Lisbon Treaty gave the EU competence to lay down the conditions governing entry into, and legal residence, in a member state for third-country nationals, including for the purposes of family reunification. Article 79 also sought to promote enhanced measures to combat illegal immigration and trafficking in human beings, while member states retained the right to determine volumes of admission for people coming from third countries to seek work.

By making its agreement conditional on retaining an opt-out from participation in the Schengen visa and borders rules, the UK could request opt-ins, subject to approval by the Schengen states (Oliver et al, 2018: 21). The UK also limited its involvement by opting out of harmonisation measures such as the law on legal migration of non-EU citizens. After initially opting in to some of the measures on irregular migration, the UK opted out of the Return Directive (2008/115/EC), which provided the EU with common standards for returning persons staying illegally on member states' territories, and the directive penalising employers of irregular migrants (2009/52/EC). The 'communitarisation' of the Schengen and Dublin measures raised important issues of national sovereignty, since they implied that a decision reached in one member state about the status of refugees should be accepted in another without renegotiation. In an attempt to protect its sovereignty, the UK opted into the first phase measures on asylum law, but out of almost all second and third phase proposals.

The impact of the migrant crisis on European unity

When the other EU member states were dealing with the refugee crisis in 2015, Ireland and the UK were able to remain outside the protocol integrating the Schengen *acquis* into the treaties, thereby avoiding some of the harshest effects of the crisis. Although technically a signatory, Denmark was able choose whether to adopt legislation that was binding on other member states.

The Dublin Convention placed a heavy burden on Mediterranean countries – Greece, Italy, Malta and Spain – since they were the first ports of entry to the EU. Whereas Germany and the Czech Republic adopted open-door policies for Syrian asylum seekers in 2015, Hungary, Slovakia and Poland officially stated their opposition to any possible revision or enlargement of the Dublin Regulation, specifically referring to the eventual introduction of new mandatory or permanent quotas. While the German Chancellor, Angela Merkel, was being strongly criticised for her open-door policy, as more than a million migrants flowed across Germany's borders in 2015, Hungary entered a process of dissent not only from open borders, but also from the EU's economic and political integration project, even calling for an end to its welfare state (Lendvai-Bainton, 2017: 412).

Dublin was suspended in 2015 during the migration crisis, but in July 2017 the CJEU upheld it, giving EU member states the right to deport migrants to the first country of entry to the EU. This policy change reignited internal divisions in the EU at a time when its institutions were striving to maintain a united front in the Brexit negotiations, and populist parties were gaining support.

Against this background, at the February 2016 summit in Brussels, heads of state and government in other member states were sympathetic to David Cameron, the UK's prime minister, as he attempted to negotiate concessions for countries facing undue pressures on their social services from intra-European migration (European Council Conclusions, EUCO 1/16). What Cameron brought back from the summit did not suffice to prevent free movement from becoming a major issue for the UK in the referendum campaign and in the withdrawal negotiations, but the fact that these same measures could be applied within EU27 may have facilitated subsequent agreement between the UK and EU27 over the arrangements for intra-EU migrants post-Brexit.

Preparing for social policy in a post-Brexit Europe

When Jean-Claude Juncker became President of the European Commission in 2014, the ground had been prepared for his mandate in a report designed to complete EMU. The report was drawn up under his name in close cooperation with the president of the Euro summit, Donald Tusk, the president of the Eurogroup, Jeroen Dijsselbloem, the president of the European Central Bank, Mario Draghi and the president of the European Parliament, Martin Schulz (Juncker, 2015). The central tenet of the report, which focussed primarily on employment and labour markets, was that the deepening of EMU was essential if the EU was to absorb further economic shocks, and ensure a competitive social market economy targeting full employment and social progress. The fact that the presidents' report was written for eurozone countries would seem to suggest that its authors wanted to avoid UK involvement, and/or that the UK was already regarded as an outsider. This section considers how both the UK's stance on social policy and the prospect of Brexit may have influenced the Commission's vision for a future European social project.

Reinventing the EU's social dimension

In the days preceding the UK's triggering of article 50 on 29 March 2017, the Commission opportunistically published a White Paper on *The future of Europe: Reflections and scenarios for the EU27 by 2025*. The five presidents' report had recognised that poor performance predated the crisis, that there was no 'one-size-fits-all' template to follow, and that all member states were facing the challenge of population ageing. The report stressed the importance of ensuring that 'every citizen has access to adequate education and that an effective social protection system is in place to protect the most vulnerable in society, including a "social protection floor"'; and a strong case was made for Europe achieving a 'social triple A' (Juncker, 2015: 8).

The White Paper confirmed Juncker's intention to promote a more pro-active approach to future EU social policy, demonstrating to EU citizens that the Commission had not lost sight of their interests. He gave pride of place to social policy when he announced that the first in a series of reflection papers in April 2017 would be devoted to the 'social dimension of Europe' and that a social summit would be held in Gothenburg in November of the same year. The overall aim was to look at how Europe can deliver 'a Union which promotes economic and social progress as well as cohesion and convergence, while upholding the integrity of the internal market', as called for in the Council's Rome Declaration of 25 March 2017.

According to diplomats involved in the negotiations, the Declaration was the result of a compromise between 'champions of the social dimension – principally center-left governments in Sweden, Italy and Malta – faced off against its critics, led by Hungary and Poland'. If the proposal was timed to take advantage of the UK's prospective withdrawal to advance the Commission's social agenda, as seems likely, Brexit could be said to have contributed to the momentum: 'Not only because it made the discussion easier, but also because it highlighted the need for the

EU to show it can improve the lives of its citizens' (Cooper, 2017). For Juncker, the time had come to launch his European Pillar of Social Rights, structured around equal opportunities and access to the labour market, fair working conditions, and social protection and inclusion, which he had long been advocating.

Had the UK been a member of the eurozone, it would undoubtedly have raised strong objections to the proposals contained in the report for centrally strengthening social cohesion, ensuring greater EU-level coordination of social security systems, formalising a social protection floor, and achieving common standards for certain aspects of tax policy, notably for the corporate tax base. It would most probably have concurred with the need expressed for better recognition of qualifications. It would have been surprised to see the French agreeing to easier access to public sector jobs for non-nationals, and to observe that member states would be able to advance at their own speed.

Towards a multi-speed social Europe

Thirty years earlier, in his plans for completing the single European market, Arthur Cockfield (1994: 162), the architect of the SEA, identified four 'groupings' in EC12: an inner circle of member states who would progress to full economic and political union (in effect most of the founding member states); a second group (some of the founding member states plus Ireland and Spain) who would accept economic but not political union; a third group mainly composed of non-EC member states, together with Denmark and the UK, who would accept something like the 1992 programme but not more; and an outer circle comprising the European Free Trade Area (EFTA), who would have to accept the rules without any say in them. His intention was to formalise the existing situation. Cockfield (1994: 164–5) saw little chance of Denmark and the UK signing up to a political union, and did not know what to say about Greece. He anticipated that social security provisions would ultimately be added as components of political union. He expected most countries eventually to forge ahead, leaving the others unable to form a viable group. He saw a 'two-speed Europe' as 'neither a threat nor a possibility', but did not countenance 'the minority preventing the majority going forward'.

Thatcher preferred the analogy of 'concentric circles' and asserted that 'Where ventures are launched by Member States with limited participation, it should be open to others to join in as and when they are able to do so (British Prime Minister: 1984: 76). Her aim was to restrain moves towards European political 'union'. In the context of enlargement, in his 1994 Leiden speech, Major rejected the notion of 'a "hard core"', inner and outer circles, a two-tier Europe', while accepting the idea that 'some should integrate more closely or more quickly in certain areas'.

With a larger more heterogeneous body of member states and in a hostile politico-economic global environment, Juncker (2015: 8) conceded that 'further harmonisation' would be involved in some areas' and 'country-specific solutions' in others. By differentiating between eurozone and non-eurozone member states, he confirmed that the homogenisation of social policy was not on the agenda.

Two of Juncker's five scenarios in the Pillar referred to 'social' standards or policy in the context of EMU. Recognising that not all member states might want to pursue his objectives at the same pace, or would be in a position to do so, he indicated a willingness to operate several degrees of social regulation. He proposed that 'Those who want more do more … [by deepening] cooperation in areas such as taxation and social standards'. Others, he admitted, were 'Doing less more efficiently … [in] some parts of employment and social policy'.

The European Commission, Parliament and Council were intent on avoiding the potential domino effect of Brexit. Marine Le Pen, the French far-right presidential candidate, had claimed that Brexit could 'bring down all of Europe', and extreme right politicians in Austria and the Netherlands were proposing to follow the UK's lead if they came to power in national elections (Sky, 2017). Angela Merkel, the German Chancellor, endorsed the concept of a multi-speed or variable geometry social Europe, as described in Juncker's Pillar (Reuters, 2017). The implication was that, even if the UK remained a member of the EU, it would not be part of the central core, which meant that it would not be able to block measures applied in the eurozone core; but nor would it be required to implement policies with which it disagreed.

Reactions to the European Pillar of Social Rights in the context of Brexit

The Pillar was criticised for its relative lack of ambition, compared to the 1989 Community Charter, and for being weak in scope and mechanisms (Deakin, 2017: 200–8). In a joint statement on Juncker's proposal, ministers of labour in the Nordic countries argued that: 'The EU must not take over more legislative power from member states', and that: 'Their [the social partners'] autonomy and right to bargain collectively on wages and other terms of employment must be upheld' (Ahlberg, 2016). An EU-wide consultation conducted by the European Economic and Social Committee (EESC, 2017) across 'organized civil society' exposed reactions to the proposal within EU27. The responses revealed the fault lines between member states in the relationship between the economic and social dimensions, national and EU competence, and in the priority areas for action. They highlighted the concerns expressed by the UK's erstwhile allies in social affairs, most notably the Nordic member states and Ireland, but also Belgium, the Netherlands and Visegrád 4 (Czech Republic, Hungary, Poland and Slovakia), which had frequently relied on the UK to vote against social measures that they also opposed.

Among EU27 responses to the EESC consultation, Denmark feared that 'the UK leaving meant that the EU had lost its centre of gravity outside the eurozone', making it more difficult for them to choose to remain outside the core group of eurozone countries as they sought even closer integration in the social field. Brexit had, the Danes claimed, 'changed Denmark's position in the EU in a fundamental way' (EESC, 2017: 49-50). The Dutch worried that a multi-speed Europe would lead to a 'fragmented single market' and wanted assurances that member states would have more say over the interpretation and implementation of the proposals (EESC, 2017: 154–6). Irish respondents were critical of the continued subordination of the social and environmental to the economic dimension and concerned to find that they seemed to be alone in considering Brexit as a serious blow to the EU. They recommended that the focus should not be on 'discouraging others from leaving, but on bettering the EU and all its facets to ensure that no other country wishes to leave' (EESC, 2017: 108).

CEE member states, and Hungary in particular, felt that Brexit exposed the various tensions within the Brussels decision-making process. Several countries rejected Juncker's notion of a two-speed (eurozone and non-eurozone) or multi-speed federal Europe, on grounds that it would lead to inequalities and social dumping (EESC, 2017: 98, 100, 191). Bulgaria claimed that 'a multi-speed Europe was inevitable or was already a reality' (EESC, 2017: 16). The Visegrád group argued that they could not accept the high costs of implementing social rights of workers, as advocated in the Pillar. Polish members of the European Parliament thought the proposal would result in 'more inequality in the Union' and was 'contradictory to the principle of subsidiarity' (Wnuk, 2017). For the Czech Republic, 'the question of [their] accession to the euro area had to be put back on the table' (EESC, 2017: 44).

The Greeks claimed that 'The increasing inequalities, as well as the inability of the EU to manage crises promptly and efficiently, have undermined citizens' faith in a united Europe.' They were sceptical 'regarding whether the results of the consultation would have any real impact in the decision-making centres of Brussels' (EESC, 2017: 84–7).

Following wide-ranging and inconclusive discussions, which raised more questions than they answered, the 'snapshot' of views provided by the Germans highlighted migration and unemployment as their most pressing issues (EESC, 2017: 79). The French, predictably, emphasised the importance of prioritising the social partners, civil dialogue, a highly competitive social market and solidarity-based economy (EESC, 2017: 72). Rather than extending EU-level competence for social affairs, a recurrent response across member states, closely reflecting the UK's position, was to demand respect for cultural differences and national specificities.

The responses to the EESC 2017 consultation primarily reflected the views of the social partners. When specific questions were asked in a 2017 Eurobarometer survey of public opinion about social welfare provisions, UK respondents were not alone in wanting less decision making about social welfare at EU level: over 40% of Austrian, Danish, Swedish and Finnish (over 69%) respondents shared UK euroscepticism. In most member states, over 50% of respondents were, however, in favour of harmonising social welfare provisions. Croatia (88%), Hungary (86%), Latvia (81%), Cyprus and Bulgaria (both 83%) recorded the highest levels of support for harmonisation. They were all countries in the most recent waves of EU membership displaying low levels of spending on social protection (see Figures 1, 2). The UK (47%) and Denmark (48%) recorded the smallest proportions in favour of greater harmonisation (Eurobarometer, 2017: 48, 51).

Given the diversity of these responses, the measured and low-key soft law approach to social and employment policy, long promoted by UK governments, would seem to offer a more effective way forward than any attempts to forge a deep social union, as pursued by Delors in the 1980s and 1990s. As the Belgian respondents to the EESC (2017: 13) consultation pointed out: 'The EU, the euro area, the Schengen area and the European Economic Area already constitute a patchwork of groups of States in terms of obligations and cooperation.'

Negotiating post-Brexit social policy

After being half in half out for 45 years, the UK's decision to leave the EU created a completely unprecedented situation. During its membership, despite its reservations, the UK had not opted out of the EEC Treaty's freedom of movement clause. On the contrary, it actively encouraged intra-European migration, particularly in 2004. A major sticking point as the Brexit negotiations began was the UK government's insistence that free movement of people would end. For EU27, the four freedoms – free movement of goods, persons, services and capital – as stipulated in article 26 of the Lisbon Treaty were 'indivisible' (Barnier, 2017). As the negotiations proceeded, and the UK government made clear that it would also be leaving the single market and the customs union, Michel Barnier (2018), the EU's chief negotiator, announced that both parties had agreed to guarantee rights of residence, social and pension rights for EU27 citizens already living or working in the UK, and rights for UK citizens living in another member state.

A motion from the European Parliament (2018) provided a clear message about the framework for the future EU–UK relationship in the social domain. Any partnership would remain conditional on the UK's continued adherence to the standards provided by EU legislation and policies. They were referring to 'social and workers' rights', and especially to equivalent levels of social protection and safeguards against 'social dumping', identified in Recommendation C(2017)2600 final. UK participation in any EU programmes would be as a third country and as a net contributor to the budget, but without being involved in the decision-making process.

In terms of its population size and its contribution to the EU budget, the UK is the equivalent of 15 of the smallest member states, contributing 13.45% to the EU's budget (Statista, 2018). Brexit would mean that the number of non-eurozone countries would be reduced to eight, thereby increasing the eurozone's proportion of EU GDP from 72% to 86% (Oliver, 2018: 168), prompting non-eurozone countries to reconsider their position, as predicted in some of the responses to Juncker's proposal.

By altering the balance of power in the European Council at a time when it has been reaffirming its supremacy, the UK's departure from the EU could make it necessary to change the voting arrangements for social policy. Following enlargement in 2004, the 2007 Lisbon Treaty had greatly increased the voting power of Germany, France and the UK. As the 'big three', they maintained 'a precarious balance of power and interests that the other (smaller) member states were able to leverage to achieve their own goals' (Dijkman, 2018). Italy, Spain and Poland, the medium-sized member states, needed to agree on an issue if they were to form a blocking minority, consisting of at least four member states, representing 35% of total population. Brexit could therefore bring about a revision of the qualified majority voting procedure (QMV) that has been used extensively for social policy measures since the 1992 Maastricht Treaty.

In preparation for Brexit, the Benelux countries were reaching out to the Visegrád (except for Hungary) and Baltic groups, which previously aligned with the UK. Their combined proportion of EU population amounted to about 22%, well short of the 35% needed for a blocking minority. Emiel Dijkman (2018) proposed that, if France and Germany wanted to avoid the temptation of dominating the decision-making process, and if the process was to be made more efficient, they would need either to operate a multi-speed Europe, as proposed by Juncker, or to adjust voting procedures to give the smaller member states more influence.

The UK's departure from the EU posed two specific challenges for the Visegrád 4 (Janulewicz and Merheim-Eyre, 2017). Not only could it deprive them of a former sceptical ally against federalists and those pushing for an 'ever closer union', resulting potentially in further marginalisation. By changing the balance of power among member states, Brexit could also mean that the Visegrád 4 might be able to play a more prominent role within the EU, particularly in the social domain, where they have not always agreed with the UK.

The Eurobarometer (2017) survey on EU social policy, carried out as the Brexit negotiations were starting, suggested that a majority of EU citizens supported the Commission's role in developing social initiatives. By helping to make the Commission aware of the need to raise the public profile of its far-reaching social agenda, the UK's vote to leave the EU may have provided the impetus needed to reactivate and consolidate the European social model. Based on a set of shared values and goals, and the conviction that economic and social progress must go hand in hand, the model depended on close practical cooperation in responding to common societal challenges, as stated in the EU's 1994 White Paper and other key social policy statements. Since the UK had not been a strong supporter of collective bargaining rights as an EU member, it has been suggested that its departure might also increase the likelihood of EU-level collective bargaining processes being established (Pecinovsky, 2017).

Evidence gathered in the period after the UK triggered article 50 indicated that Brexit would be unlikely to provoke a fundamental change of direction or the revival of a strong commitment to Delors' far-reaching vision of a regulatory harmonised European social union in the short or medium term. Nor was it expected to alter substantially the nature of the contribution of social policy to European integration in the longer term, particularly in the context of continuing enlargement to the Balkans. Rather than provoking social 'disintegration', as warned by some observers (for example Snower, 2016) across the EU, Brexit might, paradoxically, encourage a more flexible (in the UK's sense) and less legalistic approach to the coordination of social and employment policies.

SIX

Brexit, EU and UK Social Policy: taking stock

In seeking to understand what Brexit means for European Union (EU) and UK social policy, the chapters in this book have tracked the development of the EU's social dimension from its origins in the European Economic Community's (EEC) founding Treaty, through the twists and turns of the relationship between UK governments, EU institutions and other member states since 1973, to the decision in the 2016 referendum to leave the EU, and the negotiations surrounding the withdrawal process in 2017 and 2018. For many observers of the Brexit debate, not least for the leaders of the Leave campaign, the referendum result came as a surprise. Neither the UK government nor EU institutions had prepared a plan B. For some social policy analysts, the outcome of the referendum was less of a surprise for a variety of reasons.

In 1973, the UK had signed up to a common market, but not to a social union. As the European Commission progressively extended its competence in the social domain, and the Court of Justice of the European Union (CJEU) carried out its role of ensuring compliance with EU legislation, successive UK governments sought to combat the loss of control over national (social) policymaking, which could have been foreseeable as an inevitable consequence of belonging to an international institution. They used the different tools and strategies at their disposal to block or delay further encroachment by EU institutions into an area jealously guarded as a national prerogative. In the process, they confirmed the reputation that the UK had gained as an 'awkward' partner (George, 1998), 'half in half out' of Europe (Adonis, 2018).

Lawyers, political scientists, labour economists and sociologists criticise EU institutions both for being too powerful, distant, slow and unaccountable in the social domain, and for not being powerful enough (Auer, 2017; Barnard, 2017; Deakin, 2017; Lenaerts and Gutiérrez-Fons, 2017; Oliver, 2018). Arguably, it was the failure of EU institutions to provide more effective social policy responses when faced with global challenges, especially the financial and refugee crises, that exacerbated growing disillusionment and euroscepticism across the EU, resulting in a 'genuine *legitimacy crisis* on a grand scale' (Susen, 2017: 157, original emphasis). Even though the UK was one of the countries least directly affected by the eurozone and immigration crises due to its opt-outs, for some commentators (for example Barnard, 2017: 478, 483), an important factor contributing to the Leave vote was the loss of trust in political leadership at national level, intensified by the perception that austerity measures in the UK were linked to those in the EU, with immigration as a scapegoat.

In the period leading up to the UK referendum, the Commission was already responding to the observed loss of confidence by European citizens in the ability of EU institutions to resolve global challenges. Although the UK was not involved in the preparatory discussions, the Commission's European Pillar of Social Rights reflected the UK government's approach to social policy by recognising that member states should be allowed to progress at their own speed according to their own customs and practices.

In revisiting the many possible meanings of Brexit for social policy in the EU and UK, this chapter returns to the recurrent topics and themes identified throughout the book and the theoretical frameworks that have been used to analyse and explain them. It challenges some of the contemporary thinking about the relationship between the UK and EU in the social policy domain in the context of Brexit by considering:

- why the controversies stemming from the inclusion of the social dimension in the EEC Treaty are relevant to Brexit;
- how the UK's EU membership affected the relationship between the social and economic dimensions, and the balance of competences in the social domain between member states and EU institutions;
- to what extent the reactions of EU institutions and other members states to the prospects of Brexit reflected the UK's influence on the social dimension;
- what the UK's vote to leave the EU means for European social integration in theory, policy and practice.

Previous chapters have drawn on a range of disciplinary perspectives to track the different stages in the development of social policy before and during the UK's membership of the European Communities (EC) and EU. This concluding chapter focusses on how the social dimension has played out as a two-way process in the relationship between the UK and the EU, culminating in Brexit. It examines how EU social policy evolved and changed as new countries with different welfare systems joined the EU, and as external and domestic events and pressures created new challenges for the European project, contributing relentlessly to the UK's decision to withdraw from the EU.

In reviewing and interpreting these processes, the chapter considers the relevance of the analytical approaches adopted by historians, lawyers, labour economists, political scientists and sociologists to the issues raised by Brexit as the UK contemplates disentangling itself from the social policies that it helped to shape through its contribution – both negative and positive – to European social integration.

Historical perspectives on social policy and Brexit

Central to an understanding of what Brexit means for EU and UK social policy are perceptions of the role played by the UK in the evolving relationship between the economic and social dimensions, and the distribution of competences between member states and EU institutions. This section assesses the UK's contribution to the EU's expanding social policy agenda in the competition for control over social affairs from different social and political science perspectives.

Spillover from the economic to the social dimension

Social policy was narrowly defined in the 1957 EEC Treaty with the focus on the employment rights of workers, which were to be developed through the promotion of 'close collaboration between Member States' (article 118). In the Treaty, the economic dimension of European integration 'spilled over' from employment rights to the work-related issues of equal remuneration between women and men, and to paid holidays (articles 119, 120). Significantly for social policy development and for Brexit, measures to facilitate the free movement of workers by coordinating social security rights were enshrined in the Treaty under a separate title, as one of the community's four fundamental principles. By 'stretching the notion of solidarity beyond national boundaries' to migrant workers (De la Porte, 2017: 152), the Treaty can be said to have planted the seeds for future dissension and fragmentation within the EU.

Due to the persisting focus on employment as a central and legitimate concern at community level, by the late 1980s, 'social' policy had come to mean essentially the rights of workers negotiated by the 'social partners' through 'social dialogue'. The title of the Commission's directorate-general (DG) responsible for social affairs, which incorporated 'employment' from 1977, its 'social agenda' and 'social law' proposals reflected the priority accorded in the EEC Treaty to employment protection. The lack of a distinct legal treaty base meant that social qua employment legislation 'needed to be justified by reference to its effect on the Single Market' (HM Government, 2014b: 13). Proposals for social provisions were legitimated either in relation to employment or, following the Single European Act (SEA) 1986, as health and safety measures for workers. Caroline de la Porte (2017: 145), an authority on EU governance and public policy, argues that, since the reformed Treaty of Maastricht in 1992, 'the EU intervenes indirectly but strongly – as a functional spill-over from monetary integration – in social and fiscal policy'.

Based on their analysis of 40 years of European social policy, the German and US political scientists Stephan Leibfried and Paul Pierson (1995: 44) concluded that spillover did not mean, as predicted by neofunctionalists, that national social policy would be replaced by EU institutions and become an autonomous area for policy development. They argued, however, that: 'a moderate version of the neofunctionalist view of European integration can be applied to social policy development'; and that: 'The emergence of a multitiered structure is less the result of attempts by Eurocrats to build a welfare state than it is a consequence of spillovers from the initiative to build a single market.'

In 1973, for economic reasons, the UK had joined what was purported to become a single market. While supporting the completion of the common market, UK governments were intent on preventing legislative spillover from the economic to the social dimension. At the formal level, EU social policy was predominantly regulatory, depending on rules, parameters, prescriptions, guidance and constraints, as part of a multi-level system of governance (Pierson, 1998: 58). Even though much of EU policy did not dictate the detailed content of national social policies, by creating regulatory constraints, the EEC Treaty set limits on the design of member states' social protection policies, meaning that, from the outset, the social dimension would be a source of tension in the relationship between the UK and the EU.

In effect, UK governments consistently and actively opposed 'europeanisation' of national social policy embedded in the notion of a European superstate. In the early 1980s, Prime Minister Margaret Thatcher vociferously rejected the measures conceived by the Commission's president Jacques Delors, together with Arthur Cockfield, the UK's commissioner and architect of Economic and Monetary Union (EMU), for using social policy to facilitate the implementation of the SEA. Cockfield (1994) and Delors argued that a stronger European social union was needed if the goal was to address the marked discrepancies in the social and economic performance of member states. The UK government agreed with this aim in the interest of free competition, but not with the methods for achieving it. The Commission also wanted to persuade EU citizens to identify the EU as the most effective level for social policy development (Hooghe and Verhaegen, 2017: 121), an approach diametrically opposed to that of UK governments, and which the Commission opportunistically sought to relaunch in 2017 when the UK confirmed its intention to withdraw from the EU by triggering article 50.

Intergovernmentalism vs institutionalism and EU social policy

In the 1990s, intergovernmental theorists, most notably Andrew Moravscik (1998), argued that, following the changes brought about by the SEA, national governments played a central role in creating and sustaining European integration by replacing neofunctionalism by intergovermentalism. Wolfgang Streeck (1995: 415), the German economic sociologist, highlighted the importance when theorising European social policy of recognising 'the constitutionally enshrined presence of strong nation-states in an international, partly supranational, and partly inter-governmental economic order'. Events, especially enlargement, the financial and refugee crises in the early 21st century, were to challenge the uneasy balance between intergovernmentalism and institutionalism.

In line with its opposition to deeper social integration, the UK supported EU enlargement, whereas governments intent on pursuing deeper European integration were concerned that enlargement would dilute the process. At national government level, Colin Hay and Anand Menon (2007: 431–2), two UK political scientists, observed that the 2004 enlargement had recast the nature and character of EU politics, and increased the complexity of the EU. They claimed that it had altered the balance of liberal and statist voices, leading to 'a more intergovernmental, diplomatic and less Commission-driven style of integration', while also making it increasingly difficult to achieve 'a popular consensus for progress on institutional, constitutional or foreign-policy matters'. This analysis applies particularly to the social domain during the UK's EC/EU membership, as it sought to build alliances with like-minded countries in their joint efforts to avoid becoming subordinated to European institutions.

Instead of the convergence of member states' social models through upward harmonisation, as provided for in the EEC Treaty (article 117), distinctiveness and even divergence of social systems ensued as enlargement extended membership to almost five times the original number. By 'greatly complicating redistributive politics and policies associated with social regulation', proponents of greater economic integration feared that the participation of countries with less developed economies and social protection systems (see Figures 1, 2) would impose a heavy burden on the EU's Structural Funds and its Common Agricultural Policy (Pollack, Wallace and Young, 2015: 478–82). They were reportedly also concerned that economic immigrants would flood to the West in search of employment.

Two decades after his path-breaking work with Pierson analysing the highly fragmented structure of European social policy, Leibfried (2015: 263) reached the conclusion that there were no winners in the competition for influence. In his view, 'under the pressures from integrated markets member governments have lost more control over national welfare policies than the EU has gained in transferred authority', although he admitted that, by the time of writing, 'this development may have stopped'.

Maurizio Ferrera (2017: 65), an Italian political scientist, expressed a similar idea in more positive terms. He argued that the opening of national social spaces had resulted not in 'a pan-European system of social entitlements, offering free-standing guarantees of protection, but an area of free movement supported by the social protections offered by national welfare systems'. As the EU progressively extended the reach of social policy framed within a multi-level system of welfare governance, the EU had, he claimed, not become a 'social superstate' or a 'social union', a view widely shared by many analysts of European social policy.

The political scientists Matthew Goodwin and Roger Eatwell (2018: xxv, 25–9) have shown how the global financial, eurozone and refugee crises exacerbated 'the deep cultural and economic divides ... that underpin national populism', revealing key fault lines. The ensuing recession, austerity agenda and associated euroscepticism called into question the ability of established political systems to deal with the causes and consequences of populism in countries as diverse as Austria, Denmark, France, Greece, Hungary, Italy, the Netherlands and Sweden, arguably justifying intervention by supranational institutions.

Since the UK had opted out of the eurozone and the Schengen Agreement, it was shielded from some of the harshest direct effects of the crises. Writing before the UK referendum, and after having tracked the influence of euroscepticism in UK politics for over 20 years, David Baker and Pauline Schnapper (2015: 15) noted with prescience that 'Britain is moving away from the EU under pressure from eurosceptic parties and the press, at a time when British political and economic policy preferences have never been as influential in Europe'. In their analysis, they show that 'intergovernmentalism on the one hand and ordo [statist]/neoliberalism on the other are increasingly dominant features of post-recession EU debate and policies'.

To what extent interventions by the UK were responsible for preventing greater loss of control over national welfare systems is, however, a moot question. Only time will tell whether EU institutions would gain more 'transferred authority' if the UK was no longer a member state. For the Slovak historian, Stefan Auer (2017: 50), Brexit offers the UK the opportunity to escape from the EU's 'sovereignty paradox', whereby 'member states have ceded too much control to the supranational level to be able to set effective policies in important areas independently of each other and of the Union institutions', as illustrated by the refugee crisis.

The UK as a social policy outlier in the EEC

One of the main reasons why it is difficult to assess the extent of the UK's influence over EU social policy and the impact of Brexit is that UK governments have been unwilling to engage unreservedly with Europe as an EC/EU member. Edward Heath, who took the UK into the EC, was most probably the only UK prime minister to be emotionally committed to the goal of European political union (Powell, 2018: 137). The UK has long been portrayed as 'a stranger in Europe' (Wall, 2008), 'an awkward partner' (George, 1998), 'a semi-detached' (Outhwaite, 2017: vii) or 'reluctant' member state (Auer, 2017: 41), and 'half in half out' of Europe (Adonis, 2018). Less often is it described as a 'quiet' but 'constructive' European (Oliver, 2018: 2, 15, 38). This section explores how these perceptions arose and how they affected the UK's ability to operate within the EU's complex interactive regulatory system, thereby increasing the likelihood of the UK one day leaving the EU completely.

Becoming an awkward partner in Europe

Before the UK joined the EC, the French president Charles de Gaulle had only five other member states to contend with. He used his position to oppose the introduction of QMV and his veto to block the extension of the Commission's powers, making France the awkward partner. In the 1980s the French president François Mitterrand supported a strong Europe but opposed too much power being given to European institutions. He developed a 'concentric circles' vision of Europe around a core of 'advanced liberal democracies' (Guyomarch, Machin and Ritchie, 1998: 25, 28), not very different from Jean-Claude Juncker's multi-speed approach in the 2017 European Pillar of Social Rights.

When the UK joined the EC, its reputation as an outlier and its relatively weak economy meant that it posed less of a threat than it might otherwise have done to France's supremacy in a domain that was essentially modelled on the French system. The ability of the French to promote their interests, institutional templates and agendas, and to impose their conception of social policy on the EEC is amply documented (Collins, 1975; Guyomarch, Machin and Ritchie, 1998). They ensured inclusion in the EEC Treaty of the social rights of mobile workers as well as an article (119) on equal pay for men and women, as laid down in the French constitution. The reference to paid holiday entitlements (article 120) reflected provisions in the French social system. The French also influenced the expansion of the EU's social policy remit in the 1980s and 1990s under Delors' presidency of the European Commission. Following re-unification in 1990, Germany became the most powerful player driving the creation of the eurozone, the UK having opted out of EMU in 1992.

Historical institutionalists attributed the progressive loss of control by national governments over social policy not only to the autonomous actions of supranational organisations, such as the EU, but also to the short-termism of national governments preoccupied with domestic interests, the prevalence of unintended consequences, and the variability of member state policy preferences. According to Pierson (1998: 37–9), by the late 1990s, path-dependency had produced a fragmented but discernible multi-tiered European polity, with short-term goals dominating the strategies of elected governments.

Not only did the EU founding member states have in common their corporative employment-based, social insurance systems, which distinguished them from the essentially tax-based arrangements operated in the UK and the other two countries (Denmark and Ireland) that became EC member states in 1973. The UK's political and legal systems were also fundamentally different from those in the six founding member states. Commenting on the relationship between Britain and the EU from Thatcher to Blair from an insider's perspective, Stephen Wall identified an array of characteristics of UK governance that made it difficult for the UK to operate as an effective EU partner:

> A whole range of factors goes into the formulation of policy, starting with the view of the Party in power of where the national interest lies, but being constantly affected by the pressures of public and Parliamentary opinion, by events to which a response is required, by the advice Ministers receive, by the personality, beliefs judgements – and prejudices – of the Ministers themselves, especially the Prime Minister; and by historical memory. (Wall, 2013: 2)

Because of its different strategic outlook, historical experiences, political and legal systems, the UK entered the EC as 'a stranger' (Wall, 2008). Forty-five years later, it was planning to leave the EU arguably without having ever been much more than 'half in', at least as far as the approach of UK governments to social policy was concerned.

Reconciling incompatible styles of governance

The first-past-the-post electoral system and the UK's confrontational form of governance distinguished the UK from the more consensual-driven politics and coalition governments of many of its continental neighbours accustomed to a system of compromise. The Westminster-style-zero-sum-game mentality of win/ lose, compared to the consensual rule-based system of EEC6 member states, put the UK at a disadvantage in negotiations with its European neighbours (Oliver, 2018: 46). UK politicians and diplomats had to learn to present national interests in a way that did not appear to be against European interests. By contrast, the French, for example, were 'adept at wrapping pursuit of their national interest in a *communautaire* vocabulary' (George, 1998: 278). When, in the 1980s, negotiations over the number of votes required in QMV for social measures resulted in concessions and compromise, back-bench eurosceptics and the press were not interested in bargains and trade-offs since 'they saw everything to do with Britain and the EU in terms of winning or losing' (George, 1998: 259).

Arguably, British politicians, particularly Thatcher, have rarely if ever pursued anything more than 'a transactional approach' to EU membership (Oliver et al, 2018: 5; Powell, 2018: 138). The most blatant expression of the UK government's opposition to the promotion of EU social policy was Thatcher's showdown on social Europe with Delors in 1988 when he was seeking to place it on a par with economic integration. Their battle of minds provoked her 1988 Bruges speech, described as the most influential prime ministerial statement on Europe (Adonis, 2018: xiii). Her intervention was seen as 'legitimating' the latent euroscepticism that resulted in the UK's rejection of the 1989 Community Charter of the Fundamental Social Rights of Workers and the opt-out from the Social Chapter in the Maastricht Treaty in 1992.

By alerting the public 'to the fact that European integration was diluting national sovereignty', Maastricht was to mark 'a turning point in the causal underpinnings of European integration' (Hooghe and Marks, 2008: 21). It vindicated the UK's half-in half-out arrangement in the protocol on the 2000 Charter and its inexorable disengagement from both political and social union, culminating 24 years later in the decision to leave the EU (Westlake, 2017: 14; Oliver, 2018: 7; Stuart, 2018).

Another factor distinguishing the UK from most of the continental founding member states and explaining its 'awkwardness' was the absence of a codified constitution. The tensions between common law and Roman civil law made it difficult, at the outset, for UK governments to work with the EU's codified system. As a centralised state, with power resting in Westminster supported by a professional civil service in Whitehall, parliament assumed responsibility for ratifying treaties and agreeing to EU social measures rather than putting them to a referendum, as did the other applicants in 1972 (Denmark, Ireland and Norway). The French government even invited its electorate to decide in a referendum whether to admit the four applicants; 68.3% approved compared with 67.2% of UK voters in the 1975 referendum on whether to remain. Norway's electorate voted against joining the EC.

The French and Dutch electorates rejected the EU's Constitutional Treaty in 2004, prompted in the French case by fears that deeper integration would undermine the national social model (Binzer Hobolt and Brouard, 2011: 319). The first Irish referendum on the 2007 Lisbon Treaty produced a negative vote, which was reversed after concessions were granted on social issues. Denmark voted in referendums against proposals for treaty changes and legislation in the social domain and negotiated opt-outs to persuade the Danish public to change their votes.

Due to the supremacy of its parliament's decision-making powers, the UK did not have detailed and explicit rules and regulations for holding referendums and implementing their results. This difference called into question the legitimacy of using the referendum as a decisive rather than a consultative device, and of basing the momentous decision to leave the EU on a narrow margin of votes. Legal and political opinion was divided as to whether the 2016 referendum was advisory or binding (Fullfact, 2016). Vernon Bogdanor (2018), the UK constitutional historian, argued that, by treating the referendum result as decisive: 'The sovereignty of the people is coming to trump the sovereignty of parliament', creating what could be seen as a third chamber of parliament. Accordingly, he reasoned that the people should be given an opportunity to vote in a second referendum on the outcome of the Brexit negotiations. Bogdanor's view was supported by legal and constitutional experts, as well as by politicians, while acknowledging that another 'people's vote' would require parliamentary approval.

The UK's ambivalent influence on EU social integration

If, as Ferrera (2017: 50) suggests, the social domain is characterised by 'the asymmetry between negative and positive integration, market-making and market-correcting, EU (economic and legal) powers and national sovereignty', the UK can be considered to have been most often a negative integrator, due to the reluctance of its governments to engage with EU institutions in supporting social policy initiatives. By contrast, France could be characterised during the years of UK membership as a driver of positive social integration. The analysis in this book shows that, although the UK played no part in shaping the social dimension as originally enshrined in the EEC Treaty, and consistently opposed the europeanisation of social policy, UK officials, lobbyists and social scientists made an important contribution to European social policy development. They helped to craft more palatable alternatives to hard law and the harmonisation of welfare systems, and proffered examples of best practice across an expanding range of social provisions. This section considers how, with support from other member states, UK governments used their ambivalent position to restrain the actions of EU institutions, while other UK actors assisted the Commission in extending the reach of EU social law well beyond the EEC Treaty's provisions.

Restraining EU social policy initiatives

Whereas the chapter on social policy in the EEC Treaty made limited provisions for workers to ensure a 'level playing field', the Treaty laid down arrangements for issuing directives or regulations 'necessary to effect progressively the free movement of workers' (article 49). The UK, backed by other EU governments, succeeded in retaining unanimous voting for the harmonisation of social security systems for migrant workers (article 51), but it could not revoke the regulations already enshrined in the *acquis*, which were to have important implications for the 2016 referendum campaign and future social policy engagement.

While the Commission was able to use the free movement and equal pay articles to extend EU competence in the social domain, due to the relatively weak regulatory base in other areas of social policy, the EEC Treaty's social dimension developed by fits and starts, with 'spurts' of activity at different stages (Daly 2017: 97–8). Prompted by 'policy entrepreneurs' (Kingdon, 1995), and in consultation with the European Economic and Social Committee (EESC), the Commission, which had itself been described as a 'policy entrepreneur' (Rhodes, 1995: 85–6), successfully brought forward major social policy initiatives, many of which UK governments sought to derail.

The first significant EU-level spurt was the 1974 social action programme, coinciding with the membership of Denmark, Ireland and the UK, suggesting that their entry provided an incentive for developing the social dimension. During his appointment at the Commission, Michael Shanks (1973), a UK national, helped to launch the programme. With the notable exceptions of directives on equal pay and treatment for women and men, little progress was made in implementing social policy proposals for a decade, due not only to the Treaty's limited legal provisions but also to the prevailing economic and political climate.

Under Delors' three mandates as president of the Commission (1985–94), social policy (for workers) became a central concern. The UK government's failure to prevent QMV from being extended in the SEA beyond the provisions originally envisioned meant that a raft of directives in the social domain, hitherto blocked or delayed using its veto, could be adopted. Delors' proposals found expression in the 1989 Community Charter, which he projected as the social dimension of the 1992 Maastricht Treaty. The UK's opt-out meant that the Charter, with the non-binding status of a social chapter, was annexed to the Treaty together with a protocol, effectively removing the UK from the negotiating table, establishing it as a rule-taker rather that a rule-maker.

The next social policy spurt was the far-reaching 1994 White Paper, *European social policy: A way forward for the Union* (COM(94)333 final), issued by the Commission during the UK's opt-out. The White Paper confirmed the importance of multi-level/multi-faceted cooperative governance in promoting dialogue between political (member states), social (employers and unions) and civil (non-governmental) partners. Although the UK opposed shifting more influence to the social partners, it could not prevent them from acquiring the power to initiate framework directives. Despite its reputation for hindering the progress of social legislation, the White Paper recorded the UK, with Portugal, as having the best record for transposing employment and social policy directives at that time.

Reviving UK influence over EU social policy

Tony Blair's third way Labour government in 1997 opted into the Social Chapter, allowing it to be incorporated into the Treaty of Amsterdam. Blair was supportive of the Commission's open method of coordination (OMC), introduced initially in 1998 as a tool for achieving the targets set for the European Employment Strategy (EES). For Blair, OMC afforded a welcome alternative to hard law by focussing on measures to support employment growth, which he saw as an area of legitimate EU-level competence. OMC was based on the principles of subsidiarity, convergence through concerted action, mutual learning, and management by objectives, with targets set by national governments, all of which chimed with the approach of the UK government. Blair used the opportunity to demonstrate how member states could upload policies based on national preferences and resources (Hopkin and Van Wijnbergen, 2011: 275). For Simon Deakin (2017: 198, 200), a UK specialist in labour law, soft law meant a loss of opportunity for EU social law. He claimed that the OMC shifted the debate from '"legislative deadlock" to outright conflict between the goals of labour protection and market integration, resulting in the further subordination of social policy to an ultra-liberal conception of market integration'.

The introduction of OMC meant that EU intervention in social policy could be extended to all areas of social life without being blocked by recalcitrant member states. By the early 2000s, the OMC encompassed working conditions, education, training and research, wider gender issues and other forms of discrimination, social inclusion, non-work related social security provisions, public health and social care for all citizens. These were areas in which UK social scientists offered the Commission considerable expertise, particularly in evidence-based policy and practice, as recounted in Chapter 3.

The 2000 Charter, another significant social policy spurt, flagged in the 1994 White Paper, legitimated this extension of EU social policy development well beyond the workplace. The Charter required respect for 'national laws governing the exercise of such freedom and right' in the case of education (article 14), whereas for social security and social assistance rights were to be exercised 'in accordance with the rules laid down by Community law and national laws and practices' (article 34). Aware of the loopholes, and despite seeming 'concessions', the UK (with Poland) negotiated a clarifying opt-out from the Charter, meaning that the CJEU could not take precedence over national courts in resolving any disputes, but simultaneously limiting the UK's ability to influence arrangements at EU level.

Legal analysts (for example Lenaerts and Gutiérrez-Fons, 2017: 434) argue that the 2000 Charter showed how 'EU social law has outgrown its internal market origins, to the point where it now contributes to defining the very nature of EU law itself'. The

Charter was excluded from retained law in the UK's European Union (Withdrawal) Act 2018 (Cowie, 2018: 34). Close scrutiny of EU social law suggests, however, that it is not as all-encompassing as national legal provisions for social insurance, public assistance, health and welfare services and housing, which remain within the competence of member states. Nor can EU institutions intervene in matters of pay, the right of association, the right to strike or to impose lock-outs (2009 Treaty on the Functioning of the EU, article 153), which the UK consistently opposed.

A major spurt post-2012 was the development of the Social Investment Package (SIP), culminating in Juncker's European Pillar of Social Rights in 2017. As in previous policy statements, in Recommendation C(2017)2600 final, the Commission made clear that the Pillar was designed to promote social policy as a productive factor by reintegrating it into the evolving process of EMU in the eurozone countries. The social dimension thus continued to have a 'market-constituting' function. The Pillar was also intended to reduce inequality, maximise job creation and enhance human capital. Social policy could thus be presented as an input into sustainable economic development and a function of it rather than simply the result of market integration.

The UK was not consulted on the proposal since the results of the UK referendum were known by the time the Pillar was announced. The UK's influence could, nonetheless, be felt (the elephant in the room) in the attention paid in the Commission's 2017 White Paper (COM(2017)2025 §§18, 19) to ensuring that the Pillar 'does not entail an extension of the Union's powers as defined by the Treaties' or 'affect the right of Member States to define the fundamental principles of their social security systems and … the financial equilibrium thereof'.

Competing for influence over social policy

Many of the instances cited in this book demonstrate how the UK used its blocking powers or opt-outs to protect its national interests. Already in the 1990s, Streeck (1995: 417) was arguing that some governments may have supported a strong European social dimension in the 1980s, 'knowing that the British vote would ensure that proposed policies would never pass into law'. A few member states were encouraged to make concessions and appear '*communautaires*' confident that the UK would prevent a particular package from being accepted (George, 1998: 206). The limits of national competence, and of the UK's willingness to fight for the interests of other member states, were amply demonstrated during the UK's opt-out from the Social Chapter and during the eurozone crisis. Greek bailouts were made conditional on the adoption of austerity measures, requiring reforms of its social protection system and the relaxation of employment protection regulations. After the 2010 euro crisis, the UK refused to be liable for eurozone bailouts for Greece, Portugal, Spain and Cyprus, although it made a bilateral arrangement with Ireland. The UK declined to sign up to the Fiscal Compact and the European Stability Mechanism (ESM) in 2012 to protect its financial sector, thereby becoming the 'unofficial spokesperson for the "'euro-outs'"', including Sweden, Denmark, the Czech Republic, Poland, and Hungary. The UK's opt-out on eurozone reform meant, however, that it would forfeit an opportunity to be involved in future negotiations on the single market, making it more difficult for the euro-outs to have their voices heard (Oliver et al, 2018: 24–5)

Nor was the UK alone in expressing concerns about problems regarding the rights of migrant workers in exceptional circumstances. The 2016 European Council Conclusions (EUCO 1/16: 7) reaffirmed the right of member states 'to define the fundamental principles of their social security systems and enjoy a broad margin of discretion to define and implement their social and employment policy, including setting the conditions for access to welfare benefits'. Council agreed to the indexation of child benefits and the emergency brake sought by Cameron, which could also be applied in other member states.

Over time, while individual member states have been largely prevented from blocking social measures due to the extension of QMV to areas covered by health and safety, new obstacles have appeared as the European Parliament gained the power to block legislation. From a critical realist perspective, David Bailey (2017: 109) has argued that market-creating or market-enhancing policy traditions and decision-making difficulties within EU institutions (European Council, Commission and Parliament) continue to present major obstacles to social Europe due in part to the large number of veto players within these institutions.

To be effective the Commission still needs the support of member states. Lawyers Koen Lenaerts and José Gutiérrez-Fons (2017: 456) conclude that: 'Democracy in a multilevel system of governance must be driven by a mutually reinforcing relationship whereby democracy at EU level does not seek to eliminate national democracies.' Rather, they must 'complement each other'. The contributions of UK officials, advisers, analysts and assessors to EU social policy development through their evidence-collecting and capacity-building activities in support of the Commission's initiatives provide examples of how non-governmental actors can play a complementary role in advancing social progress. Whether the Commission would continue to welcome this form of advice and support from UK nationals in a post-Brexit Europe remains a hypothetical question.

The social dimension in the withdrawal negotiations and beyond

The US sociologist Harry Dahms (2017: 188–9) has described Brexit as 'a multilayered and multidimensional phenomenon, at the intersection of many social, political, economic, and cultural forces, processes and corresponding fault and conflict lines', making it difficult to analyse and explain in sociological terms. In addition, not only did the underlying differences in approach to governance determine the UK's relationships with EU institutions and other governments during membership of the EC/EU, but they also influenced the way the UK handled the Brexit negotiations. This concluding section attempts to make sense of how various EU and UK perspectives on social policy influenced the conduct and content of the withdrawal negotiations and the prospects for future social policy collaboration and development.

Managing the withdrawal negotiations

In the social domain, by taking back control (May, 2018), Brexit meant repatriating the accumulated body of social legislation governing workers' rights and control over the UK's social welfare system, which, as argued in this book, the UK had never completely relinquished. More specifically for the UK government and the electorate, it meant taking back control over the number of intra-European migrants by putting an end to freedom of movement of persons, in contravention of one of the EU's fundamental principles, which the UK had used to its advantage.

In only the second referendum on Europe, in 2016 the UK electorate voted by a narrow margin to leave what had grown from being a common market to become an increasingly political and social union, founded on 'an ever closer union among European peoples' (1957 EEC Treaty preamble). The government's perpetual struggle to overcome the enduring deep-seated divisions between and within the UK's political parties over Europe considerably weakened its bargaining position in the face of EU27's alleged unity as the UK government sought to carry out what Westminster interpreted as 'the will of the people', based on the result of what was construed to be a 'decisive' referendum.

The Brexit withdrawal negotiations focussed primarily on trade and the 'economic partnership' that the government was intending to develop. In adopting its customary adversarial rather than a consensus-seeking approach, and in an attempt to secure the support of hard-line Brexiteers, red lines were laid down on migration. The 2017 White Paper restated that freedom of movement would end and that EU migration would be brought under UK law (1.4.1). In the initial stages of the negotiations, EU27 made clear that any attempts by the UK to 'cherry pick' aspects of membership in the national interest would be firmly rejected. EU27 were determined to play by the rules and prevent the UK from being better off outside the EU than it was when half in.

Although agreement was reached over arrangements for intra-European migrants already living and working in another member state, the expectation was that, in a post-Brexit EU, mobile workers and their families from another member states would be treated as third-country immigrants. By late 2018, with falling numbers of EU migrants arriving in the UK, intra-European migration, which had been a central theme in the referendum campaign, had all but disappeared from the debate and from media coverage. As far as EU27 were concerned, the Irish border was the only remaining sticking point (Barnier, 2018). For other member states, the UK was again proving to be awkward, and more important domestic challenges had already replaced Brexit on national social agendas.

At a summit in Brussels on 25 November 2018, EU27 heads of state and government endorsed the Withdrawal Agreement and Political Declaration negotiated with the UK, setting out the framework for the future relationship between EU27 and the UK, as and when it left the EU. The Agreement provided detailed proposals for satisfying the requirements of article 50. In substance, the proposals in the social domain closely mirrored the arrangements contained in the 2017 and 2018 White Papers. Whereas the EU negotiators were seeking to drive forward and complete the process before the May 2019 European Parliament elections, the UK cabinet, political parties and public remained deeply divided over the entire Brexit process.

The postponement of the 'meaningful vote', which was due to be held in parliament on 11 December 2018, cast doubts over the government's ability to pursue the negotiations with Brussels and to implement the country's withdrawal from the EU. It reignited the debate about the legitimacy of holding a second referendum and revoking article 50, and it raised the spectre of a 'no deal'.

Social policy in post-Brexit Europe and the UK

The Brexit decision came at a critical juncture in the development of European integration, provoking diverging interpretations of its implications for future social policy. On the one hand was the prospect of the EU unravelling, with the UK's vote triggering similar referendums elsewhere in the EU, perhaps even provoking the Union's disintegration (Webber, 2014); on the other hand, was the possibility that the UK's withdrawal could lead to the strengthening of the EU by facilitating 'a renegotiation and reimagining of the European project' (Kennett, 2017: 441).

Taking stock of the evidence assembled in this book, it seemed unlikely at the time of writing that the EU would 'disintegrate' because of the UK's withdrawal, particularly if it could be demonstrated that EU institutions were able to improve the lives of their citizens and satisfy their aspirations. The threat of Brexit was one of several 'shocks' that provided an incentive for a more proactive EU social policy. From a German political scientist's perspective, Antje Wiener (2017: 147) argued that Brexit could offer the 'crisis-battered EU of the 2010s' a window of opportunity to counter its 'perceived legitimacy deficit' by providing a more positive image. In parallel with the withdrawal negotiations, the Commission was already developing an initiative designed to win over European citizens, based on 'differentiated integration' (Schimmelfennig, Leuffen and Rittberger, 2015). In promoting the European Pillar of Social Rights, the Commission recognised differences in political willingness, wealth, identities, and domestic constitutional provisions (Recommendation C(2017)2600 final). The Pillar meant that integration could go further in some areas than in others, with some member states integrating more readily than others, as was already the case.

For the UK, the referendum exposed deep-seated divisions within society. The electorate took advantage of the opportunity to express their frustration over the failure of successive governments to respond effectively to the challenges presented for domestic social policy by the period of unprecedented socio-demographic, economic, environmental and technological changes that they had undergone since the turn of the century. The global financial and other crises exacerbated these trends, accelerating the decline in household incomes and living standards, and the growth in intergenerational and educational inequalities, all of which were reflected in voting patterns in the referendum. Amidst the uncertainty created by Brexit, a pessimistic conclusion, especially in the event of a 'no deal', was that, in the short and medium term, leaving the EU would create more problems than it solved due to the negative impact on the economy.

Arguably, the implications of Brexit for UK social policy in the longer term will depend to a large extent on how governments manage a 'new' partnership with EU institutions and member states from the outside. Future social policy is also likely to be determined by the trading relationships that the UK negotiates with the rest of the world. But, more pragmatically, it could depend on whether UK governments take heed of the wake-up call provided by the 2016 referendum result and use reclaimed national control in the social domain to deliver social progress for a domestic audience in what could be a harsh economic climate where, as in the EEC Treaty, the social dimension is once again subordinated to the market exigencies.

Timeline for EU/UK social policy

Date	Events and legislation	Comments
18 April 1951	Treaty establishing the European Coal and Steel Community (ECSC) signed in Paris, in force 1952	Resettlement funds for displaced labour in mining and steel industries
1–3 June 1955	Messina Conference, leading to the founding of the European Economic Community (EEC)	Considers harmonisation of social policies; UK initially invited then leaves
21 April 1956	Spaak Report on the future EEC	Social progress as objective
25 March 1957	Treaty of Rome establishing the European Economic Community, in force 1958; Part Two, Title III – The Free Movement of Persons, Services and Capital, Chapter 1 – Workers, articles 48–51; Part Three, Title III – Social Policy, Chapter 1 – Social Provisions, articles 117–22; European Social Fund, articles 123–8	Signed by Belgium, France, Germany, Italy, Luxembourg and the Netherlands Legal base for social provisions; transposed into UK domestic law as a condition of membership in 1973
25 September and 3 December 1958	Regulations Nos 3/58 and 4/58 on social security for migrant workers	Rules for coordinating social provisions
15 January 1963	UK's first application to join the EEC, vetoed by the French under President Charles de Gaulle	Submitted by Harold Macmillan, Conservative Prime Minister
8 April 1965	Merger Treaty establishing a Single Council and Single Commission of the European Communities (EC), in force 1967	Greater emphasis on social dimension; abrogated by Amsterdam Treaty in 1997
27 November 1967	Second UK application to join the EC, vetoed by the French under President Charles de Gaulle	Submitted by Harold Wilson, Labour Prime Minister
1970–74	***Edward Heath Prime Minister***	Conservative government
17 October 1972	European Communities Act receives royal assent	UK membership of EC agreed by parliament
December 1972	Heath celebratory message; French referendum on new members	EC membership agreed by 68.3% of French voters
1 January 1973	*Denmark, Ireland and the UK join the EC*	Norway referendum rejects membership by 53.5%
1973–98	Hywel Ceri Jones Commission civil servant, initially Head of Division for Education and Youth Policies	Develops education policy and European Social Fund; initiates Erasmus
1974–76	***Harold Wilson Prime Minister***	Labour government
1973–76	Michael Shanks Commission civil servant Director-General for Social Affairs	Promotes social dimension as 'human face' of EC

Date	Events and legislation	Comments
21 January 1974	Council Resolution concerning a social action programme, *OJ* C 13/1	Rebalancing of social and economic dimensions
February 1974	Wilson Labour Party election manifesto, Let us work together – Labour's way out of the crisis	Proposes renegotiation and referendum; opposes further integration
5 June 1975	Wilson renegotiates UK membership, holds referendum	67.2% for continuing membership, 64% turnout
1976–79	*James Callaghan Prime Minister*	Labour government
1976–80	Roy Jenkins President of the European Commission	UK appointee; promotes regional policy
13 March 1979	Jenkins launches European Monetary System (EMS)	Callaghan declines to join
1979–90	*Margaret Thatcher Prime Minister*	Conservative government
1 January 1981	*Greece joins the EC*	
1981–85	Ivor Richard Commissioner for Employment, Social Affairs, Education and Training	UK appointee; supports European Social Fund and Erasmus
23 February 1982	Greenland holds referendum on continuing EC membership	53% against; negotiates withdrawal, left in 1985
17 March 1983	Richard speech, European Metalworkers' Federation	Reduction/reorganisation of working time
19 June 1983	European Council Solemn Declaration on European Union	UK agrees to high priority for social field
25–26 June 1984	Thatcher speech, European Council, Fontainebleau	Advocates a flexible conception of Europe
27 June 1984	Thatcher negotiates UK budget rebate	Establishes reputation for confrontational style
30 November 1984	Thatcher speech, Europe – the future, Franco-British Council, Avignon	Criticises EC bureaucracy
1984–88	Francis Cockfield, Vice-President of the European Commission	UK appointee; drives forward the Single Market
1985–95	Jacques Delors, President of the European Commission	French appointee; relaunches social dialogue
14 June 1985	Schengen Agreement abolishing internal borders, in force 1995	Signed by Belgium, France, Germany, Luxembourg and the Netherlands
1 January 1986	*Portugal and Spain join the EC*	
17 February 1986	Single European Act (SEA) signed in Luxembourg, in force 1987 Qualified majority voting (QMV) introduced for health and safety	Action in regional and social fields Unanimity retained for social security
26 February 1986	Referendum on SEA in Denmark	56.2% in favour
26 May 1987	Referendum on SEA in Ireland	59.9% in favour
19 November 1987	European Economic and Social Committee Opinion: social aspects of the internal market, *OJ* C 356/08	Recommends promotion of social policy on a par with economic policy

Date	Events and legislation	Comments
8 September 1988	Delors address, Trades Union Congress in Bournemouth	Convinces TUC to support the social dialogue
20 September 1988	Thatcher speech, College of Europe, Bruges	Rejects concept of European superstate
9 December 1989	Community Charter of the Fundamental Social Rights of Workers, adopted by 11 member states	Rebalancing of economic and social dimensions; rejected by UK
18 May 1989	Consultative referendum in Italy on the Maastricht Treaty	88.1% vote for European integration
26–27 June 1989	European Council meeting decision to launch first stage of European and Monetary Union (EMU) in 1990	UK agrees to join the Exchange Rate Mechanism (ERM)
15 June 1990	Dublin Convention signed by the Schengen countries, in force in 1997, Regulation No 604/2013	Determines responsibility for asylum seekers; Ireland and UK refuse to sign up
1990–97	*John Major Prime Minister*	Conservative government
7 February 1992	Treaty on European Union signed in Maastricht, in force 1993	UK opt-out from Social Chapter and eurozone
2 June 1992	Referendum in Denmark on Maastricht	50.7% against
18 June 1992	Referendum in Ireland on Maastricht	69.1% in favour
1 July 1992	Major and Delors, joint press conference, London	Delors states EU policy will advance without UK
27 July 1992	Council Recommendation on the convergence of social protection objectives and policies, 92/442/EEC	Recognises limits of EU social policy competence; signed by UK Chancellor
16 September 1992	UK withdraws from the Exchange Rate Mechanism (ERM), followed by Italy	UK negotiates opt-out from Social Chapter
20 September 1992	Referendum in France on Maastricht	51% in favour
18 May 1993	Second referendum in Denmark after negotiating opt-outs	56.7% in favour
27 July 1994	European Commission White Paper, *European social policy: A way forward*, Com(94)333 final	Proposes open method of coordination (OMC) as alternative to hard law
7 September 1994	Major speech, Europe : A future that works, Leiden	Emphasises flexibility and need to reduce divisions
1 January 1995	*Austria, Finland and Sweden join the EU*	
1997	Tony Blair Labour Party election manifesto, New labour because Britain deserves better	Commits to referendum on single currency; and to opt in to Social Chapter
1997–2007	*Tony Blair Prime Minister*	Labour government
2 October 1997	Treaty of Amsterdam amending the Treaty on European Union and the Treaties establishing the European Communities, in force 1999	Renews emphasis on social rights, balanced economic and social progress, and employment
12–13 December 1997	European Employment Strategy (EES) and open method of coordination (OMC)	Aim to create more and better jobs using soft law

TIMELINE FOR EU/UK SOCIAL POLICY

Date	Events and legislation	Comments
1 January 1999	Launch of euro in 11 countries; not joined by Demark, Sweden and the UK	Greece joined in 2001
19 June 1999	EU Ministers of Education, agreement on Europeanisation and Bologna process	Creation of common references and principles
7 December 2000	Charter of Fundamental Rights of the European Union ratified, 2000/C 364/01, annexed to the Treaty on the Functioning of the European Union (TFEU) in 2010	Rights to education, health, social protection; UK and Poland negotiate clarifying Protocol 30
11 December 2000	Treaty of Nice, ratified in 2002, in force 2003; extension of co-decision and QMV except for social security	Second referendum in Ireland; enhanced role for parliament
7 June 2001	Referendum in Ireland on Nice Treaty	53.9% against
19 October 2002	Second referendum in Ireland after renegotiation	62.9% in favour
30 November 2002	Copenhagen Process for Vocational Education and Training	Enhanced cooperation between member states
1 May 2004	*Cyprus, Czech Republic, Estonia, Hungary, Latvia, Lithuania, Malta, Poland, Slovakia, Slovenia join the EU*	
29 October 2004	Constitutional Treaty signed, not ratified by 1 November 2006	Referendums held in four countries
29 May 2005	Referendum in France	54.7% against
1 June 2005	Referendum in the Netherlands	61.5% against
2 February 2006	Tony Blair annual European Studies Centre Lecture, St Antony's College, Oxford	Expresses optimism about the future of the EU and its capacity for reform
1 January 2007	*Romania and Bulgaria join the EU*	
2007–10	**Gordon Brown Prime Minister**	Labour government
August 2007–09	Global financial crisis	Economic recession
3 October 2007	David Cameron speech, Conservative Party Conference, Blackpool	Pledges to leave the Social Chapter, hold a referendum on treaty change and control economic migration
13 December 2007	Treaty of Lisbon, in force 2009	Strengthens social objectives
12 June 2008	Referendum in Ireland on Lisbon	53.2% against
2 October 2009	Second referendum in Ireland after negotiation of Irish guarantees	61.7% in favour
2009–11	Eurozone crisis, leading to Fiscal Compact and European Stability Mechanism in 2012, rejected by UK	Sovereign-debt crisis extends from Greece to Portugal, Ireland and Spain
4–7 June 2009	European Parliament elections	UK Independence Party (UKIP) in second place with 16% of vote, 34.7% turnout
22 June 2009	Conservative Party leaves European People's Party (EPP) grouping	Cameron distances Conservatives from Merkel

Date	Events and legislation	Comments
1 December 2009	Consolidated version of the Treaty on the Functioning of the European Union (TFEU) brought into force	QMV extended to social benefits for migrant workers; OMC integrated
2010–15	***David Cameron Prime Minister*** ***David Clegg Deputy Prime Minister***	Conservative/Liberal Democrat Coalition
19 July 2011	UK's European Union Act 2011 receives royal assent	Lays down restrictions on treaties and decisions relating to EU
23 January 2013	Cameron speech, Bloomberg	Endorses flexible approach; commits to a referendum after renegotiation
20 February 2013	European Commission Communication on social investment for growth and cohesion, COM(2013)83 final	Launches Social Investment Package (SIP) in European Semester
1 July 2013	*Croatia joins the EU*	
22 May 2014	European Parliament elections	UKIP in first place with 25% of vote, 35.6% turnout
1 November 2014	Jean-Claude Juncker appointed as European Commission President using *Spitzenkandidat* process	Cameron opposes Juncker's appointment
2015–16	***David Cameron Prime Minister***	Conservative government
23 April 2015	Special meeting of Europe Council on migration crisis	Leads to European agenda on migration
5 July 2015	Greek referendum on bailout package	61.3% against; agreed by Greek parliament
10 November 2015	Cameron speech, Chatham House; letter to European Council requesting concessions	Explains rationale for referendum and proposal for negotiations at Brussels summit
3 December 2015	Danish referendum on converting Justice and Home Affairs opt-outs	53.1% against change
19 February 2016	European Council meeting Conclusions responding to British Prime Minister's letter, EUCO 1/16	Concessions agreed on intra-European migration and social provisions
22 February 2016	Cameron speech, House of Commons	Cameron announces referendum date
23 June 2016	UK referendum on continuing membership of the EU	51.9% vote to leave, 48.1% to remain, 72.2% turnout
24 June 2016	Cameron resigns as prime minister following referendum result	Conservative Party seeks a new leader
13 July 2016–	***Theresa May Prime Minister***	Conservative government
2 October 2016	Hungarian referendum on migrant quotas	98.4% against
17 January 2017	May speech, Lancaster House	Free movement to cease
2 February 2017	White Paper, *The United Kingdom's exit from and new partnership with the European Union*, Cm 9417	Commitments on control of immigration and protection of workers' rights

TIMELINE FOR EU/UK SOCIAL POLICY

Date	Events and legislation	Comments
2 March 2017	European Commission White Paper, *The future of Europe: Reflections and scenarios for the EU27 by 2025*, COM(2017)2025	Aims to strengthen the convergence of economic and social performances; seeks new social rights
25 March 2017	Rome Declaration, The road from Rome: Social Europe	Call for social progress, cohesion and convergence
29 March 2017	May letter to President Donald Tusk	Triggers article 50
26 April 2017	European Commission Recommendation on the European Pillar of Social Rights, Brussels, C(2017)2600 final	Lays down principles for well-functioning labour markets/ welfare systems
22 September 2017	May speech, Florence	Emphasises re-taking control of borders
2 March 2018	May speech, Mansion House	Re-confirms end to free movement of people; commits to high regulatory standards
7 March 2018	European Parliament Motion for a Resolution on the framework of the future EU–UK relationship, B8-0135/2018	Emphasises protection of rights of mobile EU citizens, and treatment of UK as third country
26 June 2018	European Union (Withdrawal) Act 2018 repealing the European Communities Act 1972 and the European Union Act 2011	Converts EU to domestic law; ensures same rules and laws apply after exit
6 July 2018	Chequers Statement from Her Majesty's Government	Reiterates maintenance of high social and employment standards, end of free movement
12 July 2018	White Paper, *The future relationship between the United Kingdom and the European Union*, Cm 9593	Details arrangements for ending free movement and maintaining high standards of social and employment protection
25 November 2018	EU27 endorse Withdrawal Agreement and Political Declaration on the Future Relationship between the EU and UK	Sets out arrangements for leaving the EU as required under article 50
11 December 2018	Postponement of UK parliament's meaningful vote on Withdrawal Agreement and Political Declaration	Further negotiations demanded by parliament of Irish backstop
29 March 2019	Deadline for exiting the European Union	Original deadline for implementing article 50

References

The Timeline provides information about the key speeches, events and official reports referred to in the chapters

Adonis, A. (2018) *Half in half out: Prime ministers on Europe*, London: Biteback.

Ahlberg, K. (2016) Nordic countries positive to EU social pillar – but want to set wages themselves, *Nordic Labour Journal*, 13 December.

Alcock, P. (2016) What is social policy? in P. Alcock, T. Haux, M. May and S. Wright (eds), *The student's companion to social policy* (5th edn), Oxford: Wiley, pp 7–13.

Alcock, P., Haux, T., May, M. and Wright, S. (eds) (2016) *The student's companion to social policy* (5th edn), Oxford: Wiley.

Allègre, C., Berlinguer, L., Blackstone, T. and Rüttgers, J. (1998) *Sorbonne joint declaration*. 25 May. Paris: Sorbonne.

Ashcroft, M. and Oakeshott, I. (2016) *Call me Dave: The unauthorised biography of David Cameron*, London: Biteback.

Atkinson, A.B. (2000) A European social agenda: Poverty benchmarking and social transfers, *EUROMOD Working Paper*, EM3/00.

Auer, S. (2017) Brexit, sovereignty and the end of an ever closer union, in W. Outhwaite (ed.), *Brexit: Sociological responses*, London: Anthem Press, pp 41–53.

Bailey, D. (2017) Obstacles to 'social Europe', in P. Kennett and N. Lendvai-Bainton (eds), *Handbook of European social policy*, Cheltenham: Edward Elgar, pp 108–25.

Baker, D. and Schnapper, P. (2015) *Britain and the crisis of the European Union*, Basingstoke: Palgrave Macmillan.

Barnard, C. (2017) (B)Remains of the day: Brexit and EU social policy, in F. Vandenbroucke, C. Barnard and G. De Baere (eds), *A European social union after the crisis*, Cambridge: CUP, pp 477–501.

Barnier, M. (2017) Protecting citizens' rights in the negotiations with the UK, speech in Florence, 5 May.

Barnier, M. (2018) L'invité de 8h20: Le grand entretien, France Inter, 19 October.

Bertoncini, Y. and Koenig, N. (2014) Euroscepticism or europhobia: Voice vs. exit? *Notre Europe Policy Paper,* 121, 27 November.

Binzer Hobolt, S. and Brouard, S. (2011) Contesting the European Union? Why the Dutch and the French rejected the European Constitution, *Political Research Quarterly,* 64(2): 309–22.

Bochel, C. (2016) State welfare, in P. Alcock, T. Haux, M. May and S. Wright (eds), *The student's companion to social policy* (5th edn), Oxford: Wiley, pp 243–8.

Bogdanor, V. (2018) Brexit broke parliament. Now, only the people can fix it, *Guardian,* 23 July.

British Chambers of Commerce (2017) Business Brexit priorities. *Brexit Principles Doc,* V6, 21 February.

British Prime Minister (1984) Europe – the future, *Journal of Common Market Studies,* 23(1): 73–81.

Brown, J. (1987) Cross-national and inter-country research into poverty: The case of the first European Poverty Programme. *Cross-national Research Papers,* 1(2): 41–51.

Burchardt, T. and Obolenskaya, P. (2016) Public and private welfare, in R. Lupton, T. Burchardt, J. Hills, K. Stewart and P. Vizard (eds), *Social policy in a cold climate: Policies and their consequences since the crisis*, Bristol: Policy Press, pp 217–43.

Burrows, N. and Mair, J. (1996) *European social law*, Chichester: Wiley.

Butler, D. and Kitzinger, U. (1976) *The 1975 referendum*, London: Macmillan.

Campbell, J. (2014) *Roy Jenkins: A well-rounded life*, London: Random House.

Clasen, J. (2013) Defining comparative social policy, in P. Kennett (ed.), *A handbook of comparative social policy* (2nd edn), Cheltenham: Edward Elgar, pp 71–83.

Cockfield, A. (1994) *The European Union: Creating the single market*, Chichester: Wiley.

Collins, D. (1975) *The European Communities: The social policy of the first phase*, vol. 2, *The European Economic Community 1958–72*, London: Martin Robertson.

Cooper, H. (2017) Juncker seeks to cement social pillar in Rome: Diplomats tussle over summit declaration, Politico (blog), 23 March.

Corbett, A. (2003) *The forces for the creation of international relationships between universities: Europeanisation and the Bologna Process*. First International Euredocs Conference, Paris: Sciences Po, 16 June.

Corbett, A. (2005) *Universities and the Europe of knowledge: Ideas, institutions and policy entrepreneurship in EU higher education policy 1915–2005*, Basingstoke: Palgrave.

Cowie, G. (2018) The status of 'retained EU law', *House of Commons Library Briefing Paper*, 08375, 30 July.

Curtice, J. and Tipping, S. (2018) Europe, *British Social Attitudes 35* (online).

Dahms, H.F. (2017) Critical theory, Brexit and the vicissitudes of political economy in the twenty-first century, in W. Outhwaite (ed.), *Brexit: Sociological responses*, London: Anthem, pp 183–92.

Daly, M. (2017) The dynamics of European Union social policy, in P. Kennett and N. Lendvai-Bainton (eds), *Handbook of European social policy*, Cheltenham: Edward Elgar, pp 93–107.

D'Angelo, A. and Kofman, E. (2018) From mobile workers to fellow citizens and back again? The future status of EU citizens in the UK, *Social Policy and Society*, 17(2): 331–43.

Deakin, S. (2017) What follows austerity? From social pillar to new deal, in F. Vandenbroucke, C. Barnard and G. De Baere (eds), *A European social union after the crisis*, Cambridge: CUP, pp 192–210.

De la Baume, M. (2016) Greenland's exit warning to Britain, Politico (blog), 22 June.

De la Porte, C. (2017) EU governance of welfare states and labour markets, in P. Kennett and N. Lendvai-Bainton (eds), *Handbook of European social policy*, Cheltenham: Edward Elgar, pp 141–54.

Delors, J. (1985) Preface, in J. Vandamme (ed.), *New dimensions in European social policy*, London: Croom Helm, pp ix–xx.

Dijkman, E. (2018) The change in the balance of power after Brexit, Europeum (blog), 9 May.

Dinan, D. (2007) The European integration process, in C. Hay and A. Menon (eds), *European politics*, Oxford: OUP, pp 151–67.

Ditch, J., Barnes, H. and Bradshaw, J. (1996) *A synthesis of national family policies 1995*, Brussels: Commission of the European Communities.

REFERENCES

Eatwell, G. and Goodwin, M. (2018) *National populism: The revolt against liberal democracy*, New York: Penguin Random House.

Eurobarometer (2015) *Public opinion in the European Union*, Standard Eurobarometer 83, Spring, TNS Opinion and Social, Brussels: European Commission, DG COMM.

Eurobarometer (2017) *Future of Europe: Social issues*, Special Eurobarometer 467. 17 November.

European Commission (1958) *First general report on the activities of the Community (January 1, 1958 to September 17, 1958)*, 17 September.

European Commission (2009) *Economic crisis in Europe: Causes, consequences and responses*, European Economy 7/2009, Luxembourg: OOPEC.

European Commission (2010) Detailed report on the implementation by member states of Directive 2003/88/EC concerning certain aspects of the organisation of working time ('The Working Time Directive'), *Commission Staff Working Paper*, SEC(2010) 1611 final, 21 December.

European Commission (2016) *Monitoring the application of European Union law*, Annual report 2015, 14 July.

European Economic and Social Committee (EESC) (2017) *White paper on the future of Europe: National consultations of organized civil society*, May—June.

Evans, G. and Menon, A. (2017) *Brexit and British politics*, Cambridge: Polity.

Fagan, C. and Rubery, J. (2018) Advancing gender equality through European employment policy: The impact of the UK's EU membership and the risks of Brexit, *Social Policy and Society*, 17(2): 297–317.

Favell, A. and Guiraudon, V. (eds) (2011) *Sociology of the European Union*, Basingstoke: Palgrave Macmillan.

Ferrera, M. (2017) The European social union: A missing but necessary 'political good', in F. Vandenbroucke, C. Barnard and G. De Baere (eds), *A European social union after the crisis*, Cambridge: CUP, pp 47–67.

Fullfact (2016) Was the EU referendum 'advisory'? 8 November (online).

George, S. (1998) *An awkward partner: Britain in the European Community* (3rd edn), Oxford: OUP.

Geyer, R.R. (2000) *Exploring European social policy*, Cambridge: Polity.

Giddens, A. (2006) A social model for Europe? in A. Giddens, P. Diamond and R. Liddle (eds), *Global Europe, social Europe*, Cambridge: Polity, pp 14–36.

Giddens, A. (2014) *Turbulent and mighty continent: What future for Europe?* Cambridge: Polity.

Gold, M. (1993) Overview of the social dimension, in M. Gold (ed.), *The social dimension: Employment policy in the European Community*, Basingstoke: Macmillan, pp 10–40.

Guyomarch, A., Machin, H. and Ritchie, E. (1998) *France in the European Union*, Basingstoke: Macmillan.

Hansen, R. (2007) Migration policy, in C. Hay and A. Menon (eds), *European politics*, Oxford: OUP, pp 329–45.

Hantrais, L. (2007) *Social policy in the European Union* (3rd edn), Basingstoke: Palgrave Macmillan.

Hantrais, L. and Thomas Lenihan, A. (2016) The implications of the EU referendum for UK social science: Post-referendum options for UK social scientists, *LSE Centre for International Studies Working Paper*, CIS/2016/03.

Harding, R. (2018) A greatly divided and united Britain: *British Social Attitudes*, NatCen Press release (online), 10 July.

Hay, C. and Menon, A. (2007) Conclusion, in C. Hay and A. Menon (eds), *European politics*, Oxford: OUP, pp 427–32.

Hemerijck, A. (2017) Continental welfare states in transition: The incomplete social investment turn, in P. Kennett and N. Lendvai-Bainton (eds.), *Handbook of European social policy*, Cheltenham: Edward Elgar, pp 169–93.

Hills, J. (2016) The distribution of welfare, in P. Alcock, T. Haux, M. May and S. Wright (eds), *The student's companion to social policy* (5th edn), Oxford: Wiley, pp 212–18.

HM Government (HMG) (2014a) *Review of the balance of competences between the United Kingdom and the European Union. Single market: Free movement of persons.* London: HM Government.

HM Government (2014b) *Review of the balance of competences between the United Kingdom and the European Union: Social and employment policy.* London: HM Government.

Hooghe, L. and Marks, G. (2008) A postfunctionalist theory of European integration: From permissive consensus to constraining dissensus. *British Journal of Political Science*, 39: 1–23.

Hooghe, M. and Verhaegen, S. (2017) The democratic legitimacy of EU institutions and support for social policy in Europe, in F. Vandenbroucke, C. Barnard and G. De Baere (eds), *A European social union after the crisis*, Cambridge: CUP, pp 120–39.

Hopkin, J. and Van Wijnbergen, C. (2011) Europeanization and welfare state change in the UK: Another case of 'fog over the Channel', in P.R. Graziano, S. Jacquot and B. Palier (eds), *The EU and the domestic politics of welfare state reforms*, Basingstoke: Macmillan, pp 254-79.

Hoskyns, C. (1996) *Integrating gender: Women, law and politics in the European Union*, London/New York: Verso.

House of Lords European Union Committee (2015) *The review of the balance of competences between the UK and the EU*, 12th Report of Session 2014–15, HL 140, London: Stationery Office.

Hudson, J. and Lowe, S. (2004) *Understanding the policy process: Analysing welfare policy and practice*, Bristol: Policy Press.

International Labour Organisation (ILO) (2000) Introduction: Social policy and social protection, *International Labour Review*, 139(2): 113–17.

Janulewicz, L., Merheim-Eyre, I. (2017) Brexit and the Visegrád countries: Challenge or an opportunity waiting to be discovered? Visegrad Insight (blog), 14 March.

Jenkins, R. (1989) *European diary, 1977–1981*, London: William Collins.

Jenkins, T. (2010) 1992 and all that (reprise), unpublished paper communicated by the author.

Juncker, J-C. (2015) *The five presidents' report: Completing Europe's Economic and Monetary Union*, 22 June, Brussels: European Commission.

Kassim, H. (2007) The institutions of the European Union, in C. Hay and A. Menon (eds), *European politics*, Oxford: OUP, pp 168–99.

Kazepov, Y. and Barberis, E. (2017) The territorial dimension of social policies and the new role of cities, in P. Kennett and N. Lendvai-Bainton (eds), *Handbook of European social policy*, Cheltenham: Edward Elgar, pp 302–18.

Kennett, P. (2017) (Dis)integration, disjuncture and the multidimensional crisis of the European social project, in P. Kennett and N. Lendvai-Bainton (eds), *Handbook of European social policy*, Cheltenham: Edward Elgar, pp 432–44.

Kerr, J. (2017) An interactive guide to article 50, Politico (blog), 28 March.

Killermann, K. (2016) Loose ties or strong bonds? The effect of a Commissioner's nationality and partisanship on voting in the Council, *Journal of Common Market Studies*, 54(6): 1367–83.

Kingdon, J. W. (1995) *Agendas, alternatives, and public policies* (2nd edn), New York: Harper Collins.

Kleinman, M. and Piachaud, D. (1993) European social policy: Conceptions and choices, *Journal of European Social Policy*, 3(1): 1-19.

Kvist, J. (2017) Social investments over the life course: Ending European social policy as we know it? in P. Kennett and N. Lendvai-Bainton (eds), *Handbook of European social policy*, Cheltenham: Edward Elgar, pp 75–89.

Leibfried, S. (2015) Social policy: Left to judges and to the markets? in H. Wallace, M.A. Pollack and A.R. Young (eds), *Policy-making in the European Union* (7th edn), Oxford: OUP, pp 263-92.

Leibfried, S. and Pierson, P. (1995) Semisovereign welfare states: Social policy in a multitiered Europe, in S. Leibfried and P. Pierson (eds), *European social policy: Between fragmentation and integration*, Washington DC: The Brookings Institution, pp 43–77.

Lenaerts, K. and Gutiérrez-Fons, J.A. (2017) The European Court of Justice as the guardian of EU social law, in F. Vandenbroucke, C. Barnard and G. De Baere (eds), *A European social union after the crisis*, Cambridge: CUP, pp 433–56.

Lendvai-Bainton, N. (2017) Radical politics in post-crisis Hungary: Illiberal democracy, neoliberalism and the end of the welfare state, in P. Kennett and N. Lendvai-Bainton (eds), *Handbook of European social policy*, Cheltenham: Edward Elgar, pp 400–14.

McManus, M. (2018) Edward Heath, in A. Adonis (ed.), *Half in half out: Prime ministers on Europe*, London: Biteback, pp 87–110.

Manning, N. (2016) Social needs, social problems, social welfare and well-being, in P. Alcock, T. Haux, M. May and S. Wright (eds), *The student's companion to social policy* (5th edn), Oxford: Wiley, pp 21–6.

May, T. (2018) Trust me, I'll take back control – but I'll need your help. *Sunday Times*, 13 May, p 23.

Milotay, N. (2018) A new directive on work–life balance, EU legislation in progress, *European Parliament Briefing*, PE 614.708, 13 September.

Moravscik, A. (1998) *The choice for Europe: Social purpose and state power from Messina to Maastricht*, Ithaca, NY: Cornell University Press.

Moss, P. (ed.) (1994) *Leave arrangements for workers with children*, V/773/94-EN, Brussels: European Commission.

Moussis, N. (2016) *Access to the European Union: Law, economics, policies* (22nd edn) (online) Cambridge: Intersentia.

Oliver, T. (2018) *Understanding Brexit: A concise introduction*, Bristol: Policy Press.

Oliver, T., Walshe, G., Barnard, C., Hantrais, L., Matthijs, M. and Peers, P. (2018) *The impact of the UK's withdrawal on EU integration*, European Parliament Department for Citizens' Rights and Constitutional Affairs, June.

REFERENCES

Outhwaite, W. (2012) *Critical theory and contemporary Europe.* London: Bloomsbury.

Outhwaite, W. (ed.) (2017) *Brexit: Sociological responses*, London: Anthem.

Pecinovsky, P. (2017) Brexit and EU social policy: Uncertainty for the UK, opportunities for the EU, European futures (blog), 18 December,

Pierson, C. (2006) *Beyond the welfare state: The new political economy of welfare* (3rd edn), Cambridge: Polity.

Pierson, P. (1998) The path to European integration: A historical institutionalist analysis, in W. Sandholtz and A. Stone Sweet (eds), *European integration and supranational governance*, Oxford: OUP, pp 27–58.

Pierson, P. and Leibfried, S. (1995a) Multitiered institutions and the making of social policy, in S. Leibfried and P. Pierson (eds), *European social policy: Between fragmentation and integration*, Washington DC: The Brookings Institution, pp 1–40.

Pierson, P. and Leibfried, S. (1995b) The dynamics of social policy integration, in S. Leibfried and P. Pierson (eds), *European social policy: Between fragmentation and integration*, Washington DC: The Brookings Institution, pp 432–65.

Pollack, M.A. (1998) The engines of integration? Supranational autonomy and influence in the European Union, in W. Sandholtz and A. Stone Sweet (eds), *European integration and supranational governance*, Oxford: OUP, pp 217–49.

Pollack, M.A., Wallace, H. and Young, A.R. (2015) Policy-making in a time of crisis, in H. Wallace, M.A. Pollack and A.R. Young (eds), *Policy-making in the European Union* (7th edn), Oxford: OUP, pp 467–88.

Powell, C. (2018) Margaret Thatcher, in A. Adonis (ed.), *Half in half out: Prime ministers on Europe*, London: Biteback, pp 133–50.

Prime Minister (1982) Parliamentary questions (Thatcher), *Hansard*, vol. 6, col. 468, 20 May.

Prime Minister (1992) Parliamentary questions (Major), *Hansard*, vol. 6, col. 268, 20 May.

Reuters (2017) EU founders speak of possible 'multispeed' future after Brexit, *Worldnews*, 3 February.

Rhodes, M. (1995) A regulatory conundrum: Industrial relations and the social dimension, in S. Leibfried and P. Pierson (eds), *European social policy: Between fragmentation and integration*, Washington DC: The Brookings Institution, pp 78–122.

Richards, S. (2018) Theresa May, in A. Adonis (ed.), *Half in half out: Prime ministers on Europe*, London: Biteback, pp 263–79.

Rogers, I. (2018) David Cameron, in A. Adonis (ed.), *Half in half out: Prime ministers on Europe*, London: Biteback, pp 221–61.

Room, G. (1983) The politics of evaluation: The European Poverty Programme. *Journal of Social Policy*, 12(2): 145–63.

Rosamond, B. (2007) Britain, in C. Hay and A. Menon (eds), *European politics*, Oxford: OUP, pp 46–63.

Rubery, J. (1996) 'Mainstreaming' gender in labour market policy debates, in L. Hantrais and S. Mangen (eds), *Cross-national research methods in the social sciences*, London: Pinter, pp 172–83.

Scharpf, F.W. (2002) The European social model, *Journal of Common Market Studies*, 40(4): 645–70.

Schimmelfennig, F., Leuffen, D. and Rittberger, B. (2015) The European Union as a system of differentiated integration: Interdependence, politicization and differentiation, *Journal of European Public Policy*, 22(6): 764–82.

Segal, G. (1975) Unanswered questions at Wilson's summit, *Spectator*, 26 July, pp 12, 14.

Seidler, V.J. (2018) *Making sense of Brexit: Democracy, Europe and uncertain futures*, Bristol: Policy Press.

Seldon, A. and Snowdon, P. (2016) *Cameron at 10: The verdict*, London: Williams Collins.

Shanks, M. (1973) Towards a social action programme, speech to the European Institute for Social Security, Cambridge, 10 September.

Shanks, M. (1977) *European social policy: Today and tomorrow*, Oxford: Pergamon.

Skinner, G. and Gottfried, G. (2016) How Britain voted in the 2016 EU referendum, Ipsos (online), 5 September.

Sky (2017) Le Pen: Brexit domino effect 'will bring down Europe', Sky news, 22 February.

Snower, D. (2016) Brexit is a symptom of social disintegration across Europe brought on by globalisation, LSE Brexit (blog), 2 September.

Statista (2018) Share of total contributions to the European Union budget in 2016, by Member State (online).

Stewart, K.J., Cooper, K. and Shutes, I. (2019) What does Brexit mean for social policy in the UK? *Social Policy and Distributional Outcomes Research Paper 3*, London: LSE.

Stratigaki, M. (2000) The European Union and the equal opportunities process, in L. Hantrais (ed.), *Gendered policies in Europe: Reconciling employment and family life*, Basingstoke/New York: Macmillan/St Martin's Press, pp 27–48.

REFERENCES

Streeck, W. (1995) From market making to state building? Reflections on the political economy of European social policy, in S. Leibfried and P. Pierson (eds), *European social policy: Between fragmentation and integration*, Washington DC: The Brookings Institution, pp 389–431.

Stuart, G. (2018) Why I changed my mind, BBC Radio 4, 5 August.

Susen, S. (2017) No exit from Brexit? in W. Outhwaite (ed.), *Brexit: Sociological responses*, London: Anthem, pp 153–82.

Thatcher, M. (1975) Speech to Conservative Group for Europe (opening Conservative referendum campaign), London, 16 April.

Thelen, K. and Steinmo, S. (1992) Historical institutionalism in comparative politics, in S. Steinmo, K. Thelen and F. Longstreth (eds), *Structuring politics: Historical institutionalism in comparative perspective*, Cambridge: CUP, pp 1–32.

Trades Union Congress (TUC) (2016) *UK employment rights and the EU: Assessment of the impact of membership of the European Union on employment rights in the UK*, London: TUC.

Vandenbroucke, F. (2017) The idea of a European social union; A normative introduction, in F. Vandenbroucke, C. Barnard and G. De Baere (eds), *A European social union after the crisis*. Cambridge: CUP, pp 3–46.

Vandenbroucke, F., Barnard, C. and De Baere, G. (eds) (2017) *A European social union after the crisis*, Cambridge: CUP.

Van der Schyff, G. (2017) EU social competences and member state constitutional controls: A comparative perspective on national approaches, in F. Vandenbroucke, C. Barnard and G. De Baere (eds), *A European social union after the crisis*, Cambridge: CUP, pp 385–406.

Walker, A., Guillemard, A-M. and Alber, J. (1993) *Older people in Europe: Social and economic policies,* Brussels: Commission of the European Communities.

Wall, S. (2008) *A stranger in Europe: Britain and the EU from Thatcher to Blair*, Oxford: OUP.

Wall, S. (2013) *The official history of Britain and the European Community*, vol. 2: *From rejection to referendum, 1963–1975,* London: Routledge.

Watt, N. and Traynor, I. (2014) Juncker is wrong person for European commission job, says David Cameron, *Guardian*, 27 June.

Webber, D. (2014) How likely is it that the European Union will disintegrate? *European Journal of International Relations*, 20(2): 341–65.

Westlake, M. (2016) *The European Economic and Social Committee: The house of European organised civil society*, London: John Harper.

Westlake, M. (2017) The increasing inevitability of *that* referendum, in W. Outhwaite (ed.), *Brexit: Sociological responses*, London: Anthem, pp 3–17.

Wiener, A. (2017) The impossibility of disentangling integration, in W. Outhwaite (ed.), *Brexit: Sociological responses*, London: Anthem, pp 139–52.

Wnuk, M. (2017) European Pillar of Social Rights: Is there a joint Visegrad Group policy? Mam Prawo Wiedziec (blog), 9 June.

Young, J.W. (1989) The parting of the ways? Britain, the Messina Conference and the Spaak Committee, June–December 1955, in M.L. Dockrill and J.W. Young (eds), *British foreign policy, 1945–56*, London: Palgrave Macmillan, pp 197–224.

Zaidi, A. (2015) Creating and using the evidence base: The case of the Active Ageing Index, *Contemporary Social Science*, 10(2): 148–59.

Index

Page numbers in *italics* indicate items in the Timeline.